India's Epic,

VYASAR'S
'MAHABHARATA'

For the Youth & Kids
an abridgement

by

SHIV
SHANKAR

INDIA · SINGAPORE · MALAYSIA

Notion Press

Old No. 38, New No. 6
McNichols Road, Chetpet
Chennai - 600 031

First Published by Notion Press 2020
Copyright © Shiv Shankar 2020
All Rights Reserved.

ISBN 978-1-64678-630-5

Dedication

This book is dedicated to the memory of my parents :

Mrs. S. Kamalambal

Mr. T.N. Sivaraman

&

my Mother-in-Law and Father-in-Law :

Mrs. A. Meenakshi

Mr. T.D. Aiyasawmy

and

my beloved wife

Mrs. Rajamani (alias) Raji Shanmuga Sundaram

My Grateful Thanks

to my Creator

to my Parents

to my Gurus

to my 'in-laws' for their priceless, cultured and accomplished daughter given to me as a Gift to be my Life's Partner.

to my departed wife Mrs. Rajamani (alias) Raji whose memory we, the whole family rest in our heart and soul.

to my birth-place, Tiruchirapalli with its holy river Cauveri.

to my only son Mr. Venkat Shan, my daughter-in-law Mrs. Priya Venkat, my two daughters Mrs. Bhavani & Dr. Mrs. Gayathri and two sons-in-law, Mr. P. Rajakumar, Mr. G. Bapuji for their encouragement..

to Mr. S. Annamalai News Editor of 'The Hindu', a prominent daily newspaper, in English for his Foreword.

&

to my type-setter, Mrs. Priya Sivakumar & Mr. Mathew kutty of Robin Xerox & Computer Centre for their help.

Contents

Foreword

S. Annamalai,   **Madurai**
News Editor,   **02.09.2019**
THE HINDU,
Madurai.

"We are a continuum. Just as we reach back to our ancestors for our fundamental values, so we, as guardians of that legacy, must reach ahead to our children and their children. And we do so with a sense of sacredness in that reaching."

– Paul Tsongas, American politician

Mahabharata is one of the greatest gifts to mankind. An epic of epics, this story on the tussle between good and evil has always interested man. The meta stories in the epic story are standalone pieces of literature. Like the Illiad, Mahabharata has been handed over to the next generation through the oral tradition before it could find a Homer. The tradition of rendering stories of Mahabharata to grandchildren is still alive among grandparents in many households of India.

As a very responsible Indian, Shiv Shankar has attempted to hand over this rich legacy to the generations to come with veneration in a lucid manner. This book, *Indian Epic Mahabharata by Saint Vyasar for the Youth & Kids,* will definitely inspire our children and grandchildren in many ways.

First and foremost are the values it contains. Highlighted in this work are the lofty qualities of people living in different circumstances. In the beginning it is the abdication of the throne by Devavrata (Bhishma) and his vow never to marry. Sacrifice is showcased as a virtue throughout the epic. As the story unfolds, we come across several instances of Kunti, Karna, Yudhishtira, Arjuna and Drona upholding values while in the horns of a dilemma. The author has handpicked ideal instances to demonstrate that the virtuous always uphold values. This has become essential when there is a tendency among the younger generation to replace time-tested values with a new set of values that are influenced by, on many occasions, external forces.

The cause-and-effect theory, or the karma theory, is a thread that holds together the story of Mahabharata. Shiv Shankar, through this work, has sent a message to the world that it is not your birth that decides your destiny. But your actions.

One of the most profound messages this work, which also deals with the qualities of a ruler, attempts to convey is peace. It highlights how the Pandavas, the elders on their side and Krishna try to arrive at peace and avoid war till the last minute. The Kurukshetra was an inevitable event to establish dharma when all other options had been exhausted. This is a valuable lesson for the future in a world where confrontation and belligerence are considered virtues of a hero. It is otherwise.

A young reader will find the book very interesting because of the manner in which events have been telescoped. It is not very easy to compress one lakh verses in a small book. It requires a Bonsoi trick to tell the epic in a few scores of pages. Yet, it has been made possible by an erudite and experienced Shiv Shankar. We can expect more such works from his stable.

From the youth's point of view, it is a thriller or an unputdownable story.

– S. Annamalai

* * *

Preface

I am placed in a position where I surmise that so many of my readers might wonder how this author again and again chooses the theme for his books (for the youth and children) form the Puranas. Yes, it is pertinent on their part to do so. These two Indian epics 'Mahabharatha' and 'Ramayana' are the two great assests of our 'Bharatha Bhoomi' (Mother country) and they are the true gifts to mankind!

Like the two great epics Homer's Iliad, and Virgil's Aeneid, these two epics of ours are the greatest treasures to the whole Humanity especially for the literates. They are also works of great art irrespective of religion, caste, creed and community. The Greek and Roman Writers too have given many great literary works to the reading public of the world.

The reason for my choosing this theme as well as the other one about Rama and Sita is this. Both these works are universal in both their nature and spirit. They are not restricted to Indians only; rather they are the masterpieces appealing to the whole mankind.

In this mundane world where almost a major part of people are materialistic, neglecting the spiritual aspects in life, this epic of India is highly valuable. The present scenario in the whole Globe reveals the reflection of people's mind, their mad pursuit of Power, Wealth, Glory and Luxury.

With the result the whole 'Prapanjam' (World/ earth) is in a bad shape – i.e. in a tumultuous condition. There are no moral values in society. There is no safety for women and children too! There is no security for our valuables and belongings. The worst part is that the plunderers not only take away people's wealth, they even kill them for the simple reason that there should be no evidence – so cruel and inhuman they are!

The Society is in such a bad shape that people generally do not have any dogmas, principles or scruples. They are only after materialistic power.

In such a condition, the only panaecea that we can rely upon is to instil moral principles in human minds. The sleeping conscience in our people should be awakened!

Here comes the succour and help form our Mythologies, Puranas and such great Epics. Let us imbibe the spirit of our Forefathers by reading these two epics and make this world a better place to live in!

– Shiv shankar

* * *

Lineage/Family Line

Pandavas

King Shantanu

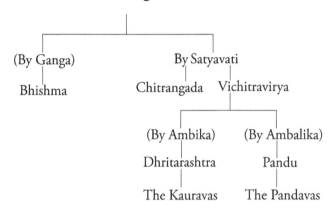

(By Ganga)

Bhishma

By Satyavati

Chitrangada   Vichitravirya

(By Ambika)   (By Ambalika)

Dhritarashtra   Pandu

The Kauravas   The Pandavas

Kauravas

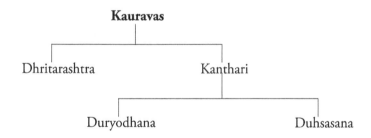

Dhritarashtra   Kanthari

Duryodhana   Duhsasana

Note:- Dhritarashtra had 100 (Hundred) Sons – 1 (One) Daughter – Duhsala

How 'Mahabharata' Was Initiated and How it Came to the World?

Lord Ganesha's Help

Vyasar was a great learned sage. He was the son of a sage named Parasara. The divine immortal epic 'Mahabharata' was dedicated to the world by the sage Vyasar.

At first Vyasar did not know how to go about the writing of this divine epic. He meditated on Lord Brahma and wanted to seek his advice. Lord Brahma appeared before him as a response to his deep prayer. Brahma extolled the sage Vyasar and said,

> "O sage, Invoke the Lord, Ganapati and beg him to help you in this great task".

The sage Vyasar said:

> "My most respected Lord, I have planned to give an important divine epic to the whole world and humanity. I have, however, a difficulty in seeking a suitable person who can take down my narration".

To this, Brahma replied:

> *"You pray and invoke Lord Ganapthy and beg him to be your scribe?"*

With this advice, Lord Brahma disappeared.

Then Vyasar prayed and invoked Lord Ganapthy who appeared before him.

> *"My most revered Lord! I have an humble request. May I seek your help and request you to be my scribe and take down what I am going to dictate. This is Mahabharata an immortal epic of India".*

Lord Ganapathi replied,

> *"I shall certainly help as you wish but I should not stop writing in the middle. So you must dictate without any pause; On this condition, I shall help you".*

In his reply, Vyasar was careful in laying down his condition.

> *"Lord! You should grasp the meaning of whatever I dictate before you write it down."*

Finally both of them agreed to observe each other's conditions.

Vyasar occasionally conceived some complex stanzas which would make Lord Ganapathi pause a while to grasp the meaning. This method of sage Vyasar helped him to conceive many stanzas using this kind of interval now and then.

Thus Mahabharatha was dictated by Vyasar and Ganapthy took the dictation.

This is how Mahabharatha was presented to the world.

Vyasar, first taught this epic to his son, sage Suka; subsequently Narada learnt this epic and told this story to the Devas.

In this way, Mahabharatha finally reached the hands of human beings on this earth.

* * *

The Epic Begins

There was a famous king by name king Shantanu who ruled over an ancient kingdom of Hastinapura. He was a descendant of the Lunar dynasty. These descendants were also popularly known as persons belonging to 'Chandravamsa'.

He was a good and just ruler. Hence people loved him with utmost respect. As usual, one day he went on a stroll on the banks of Ganga, the sacred river of the Hindus. As he was a little thirsty, he wanted to drink water from Ganga.

That was the time when he happened to see a beautiful woman. He liked her so much that he loved her instantaneously. It was indeed a love at first sight!

He became restless and his heart started beating fast. He could not erase her beautiful figure from his memory. He thought that he had never seen a more beautiful woman than her ever before.

After a while, he mustered his strength and began to speak to her.

"O beautiful woman! Are you a Heavenly being or a Drivine being? I lost myself immediately on seeing your beauty! You are bewitchingly beautiful! If you do not mistake me, May I openly say that I want to marry you at once. Please do not say 'no'; Please give me your consent to become the Queen of my kingdom of Hastinapura".

So said king Shantanu.

Ganga replied.

"O king, I shall marry you and become your wife; But on certain conditions; you must accept me as I am; you should not ask me who I am, who my parents are and where I come from; You should never question me about any of my actions, whether they are good or bad. You should never be angry with me. If you do so, I shall leave you at once for ever".

This was the conditional reply of that lovely maiden who was no other than the Goddess Ganga.

King Shantanu was so much infatuated with Goddess Ganga's beauty and charm that he willingly agreed to all the conditions put forth by the Goddess Ganga. Thus they got married and lived happily.

After sometime, his wife Ganga gave birth to a handsome male child. The Queen took the new born baby and cast him into the river Ganga and returned to meet the king with a smiling face. She smiled as if she had done a good deed and behaved as if nothing strange had happened.

Subsequently, she threw away into the river Ganga all the six more male children she bore.

King Shantanu was greatly upset with horror and anguish on seeing the devilish act of his newly married queen. He really wondered who she was, wherefore she had come and why she behaved like this in a dreadful and inhuman way.

In this manner, she killed all her seven children. On seeing the eighth child being thrown into the river, shantanu could not bear this horrid sight any longer.

Mindless of what he had already promised and although he remembered all those promises, he cried and shouted:

> *"My dear Queen, why are you doing this dreadful murder of a new born baby?"*

That is how he made his outburst of cry and anger. He boldly tried to prevent her from doing so.

She replied:

> *"My dear king! You have forgotten all your promises; You are speaking harshly to me by showing your anger; You are questioning me for all my actions. This shows that you need your son more than me. So, I shall leave you immediately. Please listen to my story before you judge me";*

King Shantanu listened attentively and Ganga said:

> *"I am indeed goddess Ganga; I am forced to do all these devilish acts because of a curse from a sage named Vashista".*

A long time ago, eight vasus who are no other than semi-divine beings with their wives spent some time on the earth, wandering among the thick trees of the mountainous forest. When they were doing so, they saw a beautiful cow, Nandini grazing over there near the sage's ashram. It was not an ordinary cow. It was a celestial cow noted for giving plenty.

The wife of one of the Vasus Prabhasa wanted to have the cow to be presented to her best friend living on the earth. So with the help of the other seven vasus, Prabhasa stole the cow for his wife's sake.

On his return to the ashram, the sage Vashista learnt with his yogic powers what all had happened in the mysterious disappearance of his favourtie cow Nandini. He grew very angry and proclaimed a curse on them. He cursed the eight vasus to the born among men on earth.

On learning about the curse of Vashista, the eight vasus were shocked and they hurried to the sage and fell at the feet of Vashista and begged him asking for forgiveness.

> *"O revered saint! Please forgive us for the wrong deed. We do no want to be born as mortals in the world of human beings. Please pardon us and undo the curse."*

Said the eight vasus.

To this Vashista replied:

> *"when a curse is proclaimed, it cannot be taken*
> *back so easily. The curse would take its own course.*
> *The vasu who stole the cow, Prabhasa will have*
> *to live long in the world but live in all glory: but*
> *the others will be freed from the curse as soon as*
> *born. My words cannot be withdrawn as easily as*
> *you may think; yet the curse will be softened to this*
> *extent."*

When the Vasus felt a little relieved, they approached the goddess Ganga. They begged her to become their mother.

> *"Dear goddess Ganga, "please be our mother and for*
> *the good of us, descend to the earth and get married*
> *to a respected man. Make yourself as hard as stone,*
> *and throw us into water as soon as we are born and*
> *thereby liberate us from the curse."*

The Goddess Ganga was greatly moved with pity and sympathy and granted their prayer. Then she came to the earth and became the wife of king Shantanu.

Goddess Ganga as a mortal got married to king Shantanu and gave birth to eight children and threw into the river Ganges seven of the eight children. The king had seen this cruel act of her's secretly in a few cases and got horrified and kept silent but questioned her when the eighth child was thrown in the river Ganges. Thus he had broken all the promises; Ganga then explained that she had liberated the seven vasus in this manner from the sage's curse. But the eighth vasu would be taken away from the father for some time and the child would be returned to him a little later. The eighth child would be endowed with a divine grace and form of Devendra, the king of the Gods. This child, however, would lead a glorious life in the world. Thus saying, Ganga vanished with the baby.

After the disappearance of Ganga, king Shantanu led an austere life with self –control and with a spirit of detachment for about sixteen years.

One day the Goddess Ganga appeared before him all on a sudden from the turbulent river Ganges and addressed Shantanu who was accidentally walking along the banks of Ganges.

> *"O! My dear king! I have brought your son as promised. Take him. His name is Devavrata; I brought him up with all care and love. He has learnt the art of archery from Parasurama, the famous teacher of bow and arrows. He has learnt the vedas from Vashista. Brahaspati taught him political science. Please take him as my gift!"*

Said Ganga.

Thus saying, she instantly disappeared.

King Shantanu felt quite happy and proud over the great qualities of Devavrata who displayed boldness, courage, and wisdom. Devavrata also attained his adulthood. So the king consulted his ministers and decided to crown Devavrata as yuvaraja. The king felt that he was relieved of all his responsibilities to a great extent and he was free from cares of every kind.

The king as he was quite free went out for his usual stroll on the banks of the river Yamuna. Suddenly he felt that the air was filled with a sweet fragrance; he looked all around and no one could be seen nearby.

Soon he realized that the divine fragrance was coming from a beautiful maiden. She was earlier blessed by a great saint with a boon that a divine fragrance would always emanate from her for some service she had rendered to that great saint.

The king, after the Goddess Ganga had left him, had kept his senses well under control. But he could not control himself when he saw this beautiful woman. He was so much overwhelmed with happiness that he instantly asked her to be his wife.

> *"O! Beautiful maiden! Who are you? I want to marry you, at once!"*

Said the king.

> *"I am a fisher-woman. I am the daughter of the fisherman's chief. My father's name is Dasaraja. Please ask him and get his consent."*

So said the fisher-woman.

Immediately king Shantanu went and met the fishermen's chief Dasaraja. Then king Shantanu spoke to him and said:

> *"I am Shantanu, the king of Hastinapura. I have fallen in love with your beautiful daughter the moment I saw her. So I wish to marry her"*

So said Shantanu.

Dasaraja said:

> *"O king! No doubt my daughter also like every other woman has to be got married to someone. Your wish is indeed a great honour to me but there is one condition you must try to fulfil. The son born to my daughter Satyavati from her marriage to you should be crowned as yuvaraja and later he should become the king of Hastinapura!"*

* * *

Devavrata - Known as Bhishma

The king was terribly shocked to hear this conditional demand which he could not relish. He could not make this promise as this would deprive his dear son Devavrata of his crown; so the king became terribly sad at heart.

It was a mystery to Devavrata that his beloved father Shantanu was feeling quite unhappy when he had everything in life. But yet he thought that his heart was pining away with some secret sorrow.

So one day he asked his father Shantanu about the reasons for his unhappiness. The Father spoke about his ageing, his responsibilities and all about the uncertainties in this transitory world.

But the wise and sagacious Devavratra could easily realise that there must be some much more reasons or secret for his mental condition. On enquiries he learnt form the king's charioteer about the mental happiness that the king had while meeting and talking to the fisherwoman, the daughter of the fisherman's chieftain.

Then Devavrata went and met the chief of the fishermen and sought his daughter Satyavati's hand on behalf of his father King Shantanu.

The fishermen's Chief Desaraja was not angry at all; instead, he was courteous and respectful to Devavrata; But, he was firm in uttering his condition repeatedly.

> *"My daughter should be fortunate enough to be the Queen; I agree to this only if the son born to my daughter and your father is allowed to inherit the throne of Hastinapura".*

Devavrata could easily understand the real reason for his father's unhappiness. He replied:

> *"I give you my firm assurance that the son born to your daughter shall be the king. I am willing to give up my right to the throne".*

He took a vow instantly and proclaimed it in a loud voice.

The fishermen's chief Dasaraja said:

> *"O! The best and the most revered son of Bharata race. Nobody in a royal family could ever do a great deed like you! No doubt, you are a great hero. As the father of a girl to be married, I have my own doubts and that is; how can I expect that the children born of you would also renounce their right as the heir to the throne. This is the inexplicable doubt that troubles my mind."*

The righteous great man Devavrata could easily understand the genuine doubt of Dasaraja and he vowed again raising his arms up and said:

> *"I, Devavrata, son of king Shantanu hereby declare and pronounce that I shall not ever marry and beget children who may legitimately claim the throne; May the Heavens be witness to my vow!"*

As Devavrata uttered these words of renunciation and sacrifice, the gods in Heaven showered flowers on his head and cries of "Bhishma". "Bhishma" resounded in the air;

"Bhishma" means one who undertakes a terrible vow and fulfils it".

This name got established in practice and Devavrata was to be therefore known as "Bhishma".

Dasaraja was greatly moved with mixed feelings of pity and happiness and he suggested to Bhishma that he could very well take his daughter to king Shantanu. When he took Satyavati to the palace, the Father-King was taken aback with great surprise.

The King Shantanu said to his son:

> *"O my dear son, you are really great! You have made a big sacrifice for the sake of your father. My sincere blessings to you for a long and glorious life. Death will not take you from this earth unless you wish for it."*

So saying he embraced his son and pronounced this boon.

The wedding ceremony of king Shantanu with Satyavati took place with a colourful celebration and rejoicing . They lived quite happily for many years. As years passed, Satyavati bore two sons and they were named Chitrangada and Vichitravirya. King Shantanu breathed his last after a few years. As promised earlier, Bhishma arranged for the crowning ceremony of Chitrangada, the elder son of Satyavati and proclaimed him the king. He proved to be a successful king as he was both a wise and brave ruler.

He ruled over the kingdom of Hastinapuram very well and he earned a good name and great reputation, but as Fate would decide otherwise, he became the object of envy and jealousy of Gandarva king and Chitrangada died in a duel battle with the Gandarva king.

Bhishma now had the responsibility of making the younger brother Vichitravirya, the king of Hastinapura. As the younger brother was yet a minor, Bhishma took over the rule till the young boy grew older.

When Vichitravirya attained manhood, Bhisma had to arrange for this young man's marriage.

That was the time, the king of Kasi was arranging for a 'Swayamvara' for his three beautiful daughters; so many kings were there – the king of Kosala, Kalinga, Saubala and Vanga and a few more kings of the neighbourhood kingdoms.

People who gathered in the hall started mocking at Bhishma as they also knew about his vow.

Bhishma grew wild and he could not relish this. So he forcibly took all the three princesses in his chariot to Hastinapura. He turned to all the kings and others in the hall and told them that he would take all the three for his brother Vichitravirya. He shouted angrily and said:

> *"If anyone of you have the courage, he can very well fight with me".*

Bhishma then took all the princesses, Amba, Ambika and Ambali in his chariot to Hastinapura.

The king and Princes who were there in the hall were surprised and they all chased the chariot of Bhishma.

One of the kings by name Salva, the ruler of Saubala shouted and challenged Bhisma for a fight. As he was greatly impressed by Amba's beauty, he could not tolerate the action of Bhishma.

But Bhishma faced the challenger Salva boldly and fiercely. He defeated Salva but allowed Salva to escape without hurting him. However, he slew the charioteer.

Thus Bhishma reached Hastinapura with all the three Kasi princesses victoriously. Bhishma felt happy and started making arrangements for their marriage. At the last minute, the eldest of the trio Amba ran to Bhishma and said:

*"Ganga's Son! I must confess that I have already
given my heart to Salva. I have mentally chosen
the king of Saubala, Salva as my husband; but
even though you have been practising the path of
Dharma in your life, you have forcibly brought me
here against my wishes".*

Bhishma as the lover of Dharma, understood the feelings
of Amba; He sought permission from the Queen Satyavathi
and sent Amba safely to Salva.

On her way to the forest, she met a few sages who
advised her to meet Parasurama. Parasurama took pity on
her precarious condition and fought with Salva. At the end
of the combat Parasurama was defeated and told Amba that
he could not do anything in the matter.

But, to the shock of Amba, Salva said that he could
not accept her as he had been insulted by Bhishma in the
presence of everybody.

Thus Amba had to return to Hastinapura defeated in her
plan and was dejected.

She appealed to Bhishma and requested him to arrange
for her marriage to king vichitravirya.

But Vichitravirya refused to marry Amba as her heart
was already given to another man.

Bhishma was helpless and Amba was in a pitiable
condition.

Then Amba boldly asked Bhishma to marry her as she was deserted by the king whom she loved. Hence she requested Bhishma to to marry her. Bhishma as a staunch upholder of Dharma refused to break his vow.

Amba's pride and prejudice did not allow her to go again to Salva. She was terribly angry with Bhishma who, she thought, was responsible for the difficult and confusing situation she has been placed in.

Amba's anger against Bhishma was so much that she was determined to avenge and kill Bhishma. With this revengeful attitude, she sought the help of some brave warrior amongst the princes to fight and kill Bhishma. But Lo! No body dared to do this impossible act.

Then she sat in penance to seek the grace of Lord Subrahmanya. The Lord made his divine appearance before her ad gave her a garland of ever-fresh-lotuses. The Lord then assured her saying that the wearer of that garland would become the enemy of Bhishma and kill him.

But no king was ready to wear the garland and earn the wrath of Bhishma. Finally she approached king Drupada who also refused to kill such an upholder of Dharma as Bhishma. Then as there was no other alternative, she hung the garland at Drupada's palace gate and ran to the forest to perform her penance and deep meditation to seek the grace of Lord Siva.

Lord Siva appeared before her and said that she would herself kill Bhishma in her next birth.

Not satisfied with Lord Siva's boon, she replied that she would not be able to remember her revengeful attitude against Bhishma in her next birth.

To this Lord Siva said that he would enable her to remember everything about her attitude against Bhishma by means of another boon. The Lord further said that she would be born as a daughter to king Drupada but later she would become a man and kill Bhishma.

But Amba grew impatient and fell into a huge fire which she herself made and got her end.

Later on, Lord siva blessed her and she was born as the daughter of king Drupada. As years passed she saw the same garland and wore it around her neck. The king Drupada was scared about the wrath of Bhishma and he exiled his daughter to the forest. At the forest, as a result of her deep meditation, a Yaksha whom she met blessed her to become a male and he became a warrior known as Sikhandin.

Following is the episode that took place at the end of Kurushetra battle which has a relevance here when we learn about Sikhandin a female reborn as a male.

Arjuna then set out for the battlefield of Kurushetra taking Sikhandin as his charioteer. Bhishma knew very well that Sikhandin was born as a female and as a practitioner of his principles of chivalry, he would not fight with him. So Arjuna fought screened by Sikhandin and conquered Bhishma. The great and unconquerable warrior, Bhishma fell down with Arjuna's arrow and not sikhandin's.

At Hastinapura, Vichitravirya lived happily with his two wives Ambika and Ambalika. Quite unexpectedly, vichitravirya died suddenly. The entire family of Satyavati and the whole kingdom were plunged in grief.

Bhishma met his grief-stricken mother and said:

> *"Dear Mother, Our dynasty's future is bleak and uncertain without an heir to the throne! What steps are we to take?"*.

> *"Dear Son! Why don't you break your vow and get married? This would help us in getting an heir."*

So saying satyavati appealed to her son.

Bhishma firmly said to his mother that he would never break his vow and thereby renounce Dharma.

Satyavathi deeply thought for a while and narrated an event in her past life.

> *"Once when I was a young unmarried girl, I had to help the sage Parasara in rowing a boat across the river Yamuna. The river was in high floods during the night hours and the sage Parasara in return for my help blessed me with a son. This son was brought up by me with all care and affection. But when he reached about his fifteenth year or so, he decided to leave for Himalayas to pursue his deep meditation.*

Before leaving, he assured me saying that he would appear before her whenever she wanted any help from him. So, shall I summon him now"' said satyavathi.

To this, Bhishma agreed.

Satyavathi prayed and meditated on Vyasar. In a short while, the sage appeared and Satyavathi explained what her problem was. She said that there was no male heir to succeed to the throne. She was worried about the future of Kuru Dynasty.

"Would you please ask the widows to come to me one after another; I shall help them in having children?"

So said Vyasar.

Ambika got a son, strong but blind! Blind because she closed her eyes tightly as she got frightened by his dark appearance. Ambika's child was called Dhrithrashtra who was born blind.

Next night, Ambalika grew pale with fear at Vyasar's appearance and as a result she got a son, pale but mighty as a warrior. This child was named Pandu.

As the son of Ambika by name Dhrithrashtra was born blind, sayavathi begged Vyasar to bless Ambika again.

Ambika did not like again to go to the sage Vyasar and so sent her maid who agreed . As she was calm and submissive, she was blessed to have a wise and virtuous son. The child born to this maid was the wise Vidura but was of lower birth.

The brothers, the trio namely Dhrithrashtra son of Ambika, Pandu son of Ambalika, and the wise Vidura, son of Ambika's maid were all brought up under the care of Bhishma who had to be the care-taker of the kingdom.

Dhrithrashtra was strong but blind, Pandu was highly talented in archery and he was to be the successor to the throne of Hastinapura. Vidura was highly truthful and virtuous.

When all the three brothers grew old enough to be married, Bhishma began searching for suitable brides. He learned that the king of Subhala had a daughter by name Gandhari who was virtuous. Bhishma also learned that as an ardent devotee of Lord siva, she was blessed by him to beget hundred sons.

Bhishma met the king Subhala and requested him to give his daughter Gandhari in marriage to his nephew Dhirtarashtra. At first, the king hesitated to give his consent as his would-be son-in-law was blind. Later after some thought he agreed to the proposal as it was an enviable alliance with the Kuru Dynastry. Gandhari too, being a virtuous woman agreed but she decided to share the miserable and sad condition of her blind husband and so she wore a silk cloth around both her eyes and she never removed the cloth till the last moment of her life. Thus the marriage took place with all pomp and glory and Gandhari's brother Sakuni played an active role in the marriage celebration.

On hearing that king Kuntibhoja was going to arrange a 'Swayamvara' for his daughter Kunti, Bhishma who had already been seeking a bride for Pandu decided to send Pandu to participate in the 'Swayamvara'.

Kunti was originally named Pritha and she was actually the daughter of king Soora who was the grandfather of Lord Krishna.

King Kuntibhoja was the cousin of king Soora. As Kuntibhoja had no issues, he adopted the princess Pritha. Pritha, from that time onwards, was called Kunti.

Sage Duruvasa once stayed as the guest of king Kuntithoja. The sage was much pleased with Kunti as she served him with good care and devotion.

For the good services she rendered, the sage Duruvasa taught her a divine mantra. The sage said to her:

> "Dear child, anytime you want a help from a God, He will appear before you atonce when you chant this mantra and you would be blessed by his grace with a son who would be handsome and glorious".

This was Vasushena who grew up. He was strong and became an expert as a fighter and warrior. But he was kind and generous. Once Indra stood before him as a Brahmin and asked him to give his armour. Immediately; without hesitation he cut off his armour and gave it to Indra. From that moment, Vasushena came to be known as Karna because of his cutting. **Karna would also mean a cutter.**

When Kunti attained her age for marriage, her father Kunti Bhoja conducted a Swayamvaram. In that hall, Kunti saw Pandu as an handsome person and fascinated by his manly appearance, she garlanded Pandu. After this Pandu returned to his place with his newly wedded wife Kunti.

Bhishma advised Pandu to marry a second wife which was a custom in those days; so Pandu chose a second wife Madri, the sister of the king of Madra. Her brother was Salliyan.

On his usual visits to the forest for hunting, Pandu one day sent an arrow to kill a male deer. This male deer was a sage in disguise. He was in a romantic company with his female deer. In a fit of anger, the sage cursed Pandu:

> *"As a sinner by this act of disturbing me, you will have instantaneous end of your life the moment you enjoy the sexual pleasures of a woman."*

Pandu was terribly shocked. He narrated in detail the curse of the sage to Kunti and Madri; Heart-broken Pandu retreated to the forest with his two wives Kunti and Madri.

The young girl Kunti grew restless and curious about the efficacy of the Mantra and started chanting the Mantra.

Immeditely the Sun God appeared; Kunti did not know what to do.

The Sun-God said that he had come then because of the son-giving Mantra she had chanted.

Kunti felt shocked and horrified. She humbly appealed and said:

> *"I am a young unmarried woman and as such I would be blamed for begetting a child before marriage?"*

To this, the sun-god said:

> *"No blame would fall upon you. I assure you that you will get back your virginity after this son is born".*

Kunti instantly gave birth to a boy who was bright – looking as his father the Sun-God. This boy was born with a divine armour (Kavacham) and gold–ear–rings (Kundali).

Kunti was greatly worried about the blame and after deep thinking, she placed the child in a sealed box and threw it gently into the river Ganges.

On seeing a box floating on the river Ganga, a charioteer by name Adhiratha, took the box, opened it and found a male child. He was so happy that he decided to bring up the child as his own; His wife Radha too was happy. The boy was named Vasushena which means **"One born with wealth"**.

Hearing the suggestion of Kunti, both herself and Madri used the Mantra and both of the them successfully had the five Pandavas from the blessings of the Sun-God.

It was spring season in the forest; Pandu could not control his emotions. Though Madri was earnest and protested, Pandu was reolute in enjoying the pleasures of her companionship. At once the curse of the sage fell on Pandu and he died. Madri felt guilty and she fell into her husband's pyre and died.

Kunti and the Pandavas were sad and grief – stricken. So the sages in the forest took them to Hastinapura and they were left under the care of Bhishma.

The news of the death of Pandu was shocking to Vidura, Bhishma, Vyasar and Dhrithrashtra and they did the funeral rites.

Vyasar could foresee the dim and dark future of the Late Pandu's family and so he advised the trio-Satyavati, Ambika and Ambalika to go to the forest and lead their lives in a heritage and they agreed and went to the forest.

Pandu's five sons and Dhrithrashtra's hundred sons were happy at Hastinapura. Bhima could excel physically everyone.

Bhima found pleasure in bullying Duryodhana and also the other Kauravas; He oftern dragged them by the hair and beat them. As a good swimmer, he pushed them into pools;

Whenever any one of the Kauravas climbed upon a tree, he would kick at the trees from the ground and shake them down like ripened fruits. As a result the bodies of these Kauravas were always sore with bruises. Bhima would always make fun of them. These insults and small playful fights gave way to deep hatred in them for Bhima.

As years passed and when all the princes grew up, sage Kripacharya taught them the rudiments and nuances of archery and other various methods of fighting.

Duryodhana, his brothers and their uncle Sakuni tried all sorts of methods to eliminate Bhima permanently from this earth. They poisoned Bhima's food and he fainted and fell down. Then they threw him into the river. They planted sharp spikes on the way where Bhima would likely to walk, But luckily Bhima was not hurt as there was no spike where he fell. The poison mixed with food by Duryodhana did not work effectively as it was counteracted by the snakes in the water; Thus Bhima escaped from all dangers caused by Duryodhana; He thought that Bhima would have already died.

But later on when he saw Bhima alive, his envy and jealousy grew by leaps and bounds.

Yudhishtira and his mother Kunti warned Arjuna, Nakula and Sahadeva about all dangers that might likely be caused by Duryodhana and his brothers.

Both Kaurava and Pandava princes were taught martial arts by Kripacharya; Bhishma wanted to give more advanced training in martial art to both Kaurava and Pandava Princes.

Surprisingly he came across one sage by name Dronachariar otherwise known as Drona.

Drona was the son of Bharadwaja, a Brahmin sage. The king of Panchala had a son by name Drupada. He and Drona were close friends during childhood. Drupada often used to say that he would give half of his kingdom when he would become heir to the throne of Panchala.

Drona who had married one of the twin sisters of Kripacharya by name Kripi gave birth to a son who was named Aswathamma. Aswathamma was the pet child of Drona and Kripi; Drona was so poor that he could not give his wife and son a good life.

So he went and met Parasurama for help. Parasurama could not give any kind of wealth, as he had already distributed all his wealth. So he decided to teach Drona the use of all weapons which Drona accepted willingly.

Drona's poverty got worsened and so he decided to meet his old friend Drupada, currently the King of Panchala for some help.

To Drona's surprise and shock, Drupada insulted him saying that he (Drona) cannot expect friendship between himself-a king and a beggar-like Drona.

Drona was greatly upset and he decided to wreak vengeance on Drupada. Then he went to Hastinapura in order to meet Bhishma who was quite happy. Bhishma requested him to teach the skill of archery to the princes.

In the first class itself, the great Dronachariar informed all his pupils that he would ask for an unsual 'Guru Dakshina'. (Dakshina' in Sanskrit means a sort of fee or gift as a mark of respect and gratitude to a Master who imparted knowledge).

When alomost all the princes hesitated, Arjuna was the only one who gave his consent at once. The Guru, Dronachariar was immensely pleased and he decided instanteneously to give him specially additional training which he had given only to his own son Aswathamma.

When Dronachariar felt that he had completed all his lessons on the art of archery, he decided to test the knowldege of all his pupils. He fixed an artificial bird on a tall branch of a tree. Then he said that the princes, one by one should take up their bows, and relase an arrow to hit the head of the bird. But before that, they must answer his question.

First came Yudhishtira; Drona said:

> *"What do you see? Tell me first."*

Yudhishtira said:

> *"I see the tree, the bird, you, my brothers and my cousins".*

Then he called all the other princes who said the same.

Lastly Arjuna appeared and Dronachariar asked the same question.

Arjuna replied immediately:

"I see the head of the bird".

When Dronachariar asked him to shoot at the bird, he did so and the bird's head alone fell on his feet. Dronachariar embraced him and greatly appreciated him for his supreme skill.

Fig 1: Arjuna is having a bow in his hand

Later on a different occasion, the Guru went along with all the princes for a bath in the Ganges. A fierce crocodile caught Dronachariar's leg and he shouted for help. All the princes were in great shock but no body dared to help their master. It was only Arjuna who acted swiftly and sent his arrows five times and killed the crocodile. Drona was very happy to have made Arjuna a great archer. He was also proud of his pupil Arjuna.

* * *

The Story of Ekalavya

Ekalavya belonged to a tribal family living in the forest near Hastinapura. Even from his youth, he developed a good skill in the use of bow and arrows. He wanted to improve his skill further under the guidance of a Guru (Master). When he heard about Dronachariar, he desired to become his pupil.

When he approached Dronachariar, he categorically said that he would not take him as a pupil because he was not a person of royal birth. But Ekalavya was very firm in having Dronachariar as his Guru.

Because of his deep devotion and persistence in having only Dronacharior as his Guru, he made a statue of Dronachariar out of mud, placed fresh flowers around his neck and prostrated before he would start practising.

Pandava and Kaurava princes were astonished while hunting, to see their dog's sudden stopping of barking. The dog's mouth was filled all around with arrows but it was not hurt.

Arjuna met a boy nearby and asked him,

"Are you the person who shot the arrows into the dog's mouth? Who are you? And who is your Guru?"

"I am a tribal boy; my name is Ekalavya and my Guru is Dronachariar."

Arjuna was surprised when he heard this. Inwardly he was a little upset and angry with his Master, Dronachariar; However, he took the boy to his Master who was greatly impressed with the boy's skill and ease. When the boy said that he was practising before Drono's mud statue, all the time imagining that his great Master was guiding him.

At the end, Dronachariar said to Ekalavya:

"O! the tribal boy; when you say that I am your Guru, you should give me, "Guru Dakshina" (a gift for the Guru).

"My Master! Whatever you want, you can ask me now; I will be pleased to give you atonce!"

"Ekalavya, I want your right thumb as my "Dakshina" a kind of fee offering to the master given with devotion".

Immediately, he cut off his right thumb and placed the bleeding thumb at Dronacharia's feet. He then offered his respects, prostrating before the Guru who blessed him heartily and left.

The Pandava Princess and Kaurava princes learnt the use of bow and arrows first from Kripachariar and next from Dronachariar.

Kunti Devi had a son by name Radheya whose father was Surya, the Sun God. Kunti Devi, in order to avoid any scandal or censure kept the infant son in a wooden casket and threw it gently into the river Ganges. On noticing the floating casket, a charioteer named Adhiratha and his wife Radha took the infant boy to their house and brought up this boy with great care and love.

From the childhood Radheya showed great interest in the use of bow and arrows. When he grew up, he desired to have a good training under a good Master.

As he had already heard about Dronacharia's greatness, he approached him with all humility and reverence. But to his surprise, Dronacharia turned down his request saying that he would not teach the art of archery generally to the people of low birth.

Radheya was utterly disappointed. Then he decided to approach Parasurama under the disguise of a Brahmin. He met Parasurama and begged him humbly.

To the surprise of his Master, Radheya mastered the skill in archery quickly including the powerful "Brahmastra" which denotes an irresistible divine weapon, the one given by Lord Brahma himself.

Prasurama, the great Guru felt a great admiration for Radheya and said:

> *"I am happy to see your dexterity and concentration in the use of archery and other weapons. I appreciate your devotion and honesty. Try to practice 'Dharma' in all your actions".*

Saying so he wanted to rest a while under a tree.

> *"Please, Master! lay your head on my lap as a pillow and take rest."*

Radheya with true devotion sat motionless for the simple reason that master should not be disturbed in his sleep.

A beetle, all on a sudden came flying and stung the thigh of Radheya. The beetle was none but the Lord Indra. He had a terrible plain and blood started oozing from the wound. Radheya, not willing to disturb his master endured the pain without any crying sound. The warm blood, however, dripped on his master's face and woke him. The great master could easily realize the position. He grew wild and shouted:

> *"you have intentionally told me a lie and learnt the art from me. A Kshatriya alone can endure such a great pain. I could only curse you for cheating me".*

> *"Master! Please pardon me, like a father forgiving his child, please have mercy on me and forgive me"*

But Parasurma was angry and said:

> *"you won't be able to remember the mantra to use the Brahmastra at a most opportune moment"*

Radheya was shocked and fainted. Afterwards when he left the place, on his way he shot his arrow at a seemingly wild animal; lo! It was not a wild animal but a cow. This cow was the only asset to its owner, an old Brahmin. He became very angry and shouted:

> *"O! archer. The only asset I had was this cow. You have killed my cow which did not do any harm to you. I am very much upset. Take this curse from me. At the most opportune time in the battlefield, your chariot's wheel would get stuck in the ground; when you are weak and helpless, your direst enemy will kill you."*

Kripachariar and Dronachariar were the two masters who taught the use of bow and arrows to both Pandavas and Kauravas and other martial weapons. As a satisfied Guru, Dronachariar wanted to arrange for an exhibition to show their skill in the use of different weapons in the presence of the Royal family as well as the public.

For this purpose he wanted to seek permission from Bhishma.

> *"yes! The people of Hestinapura as well as the Royal family members would certainly be happy to see their skills."*

Said Bhishma.

A suitable venue was selected; a stadium was constructed and a gallery was provided; at the inaugural function, trumpets were sounded, drums were beaten to announce the coming of the participants and their Gurus. Then Kripacharya, Dronacharya and Aswathamma appeared on the stage situated centrally and waved their hands to the spectators quite happily.

"Dear spectators! I am glad to inform you all that my disciples will exhibit their talents as archers."

So announced Dronachariar. There was a loud cheer welcoming the participants.

The blind king Dhrithrashtra was informed of all happenings minute-to-minute that took place by Vidura. Likewise the blind-folded Gandhari was also informed of all that was happening by Kunti Devi.

Yudhishtira led the princes who were participants, and who showed their respects to their Gurus, greeting them with all reverence. Then they all began to show their skills in the use of many weapons.

A fight between Bheema and Duryodhana took place. The duel fight with the mace was fierce. When the fight between the two grew more and more violent, Dronachariar instructed his son Aswathamma to put an end to the mace – fighting.

Next Dronachariar invited Arjuna to appear on the stage. The whole place roared with cheers and applause. Dhrithrashtra asked Vidura:

> *"What's the matter? Why is the crowd making so much of noise?"*

> *"It's because they are happy to see the versatile archer Arjuna on the stage"*

said Vidura.

When the show began, Arjuna displayed his mighty skill as an archer. The whole crowd shouted happily.

> *"Arjuna is the best archer and warrior of all times!."*

Almost at the end of the day's event, all on a sudden there appeared on the arena, a stalwart looking to be a mighty warrior and all the spectators turned to look at this divine-like youth. He cast a proud look all around the crowd and began to address Arjuna:

> *"Arjuna! shall we meet, each other in a single combat? I shall prove to be a greater archer and a fighter than you."*

With the permission of Dronachariar, the event was about to begin. Duryodhana was very happy to see Radheya who was no other than his friend Karna.

Dronachariar, a well-versed master fully conversant with the rules and regulations of all sports like fight and combat, instructed and said to Karna.

"O! Karna! As per the rules, your lineage is to be known. Only princes of Royal blood can participate in this combat" said Dronachariar.

Karna was horrified and felt insulted.

Duryodhana immediately stood forward and said:

"If that were the formality, let me untie this knot and give a solution. Instantaeously, let me crown Karna as the King of Anga".

Very soon all the rites and rituals were performed, the crown was placed on Karna's head and thus Karna was made the king of Anga.

Adhiratha the charioteer, the foster-father of Karna entered the arena and embraced his son with love and affection.

Indra, the king of Gods was filled with joy. Indra in his disguise as a Brahmana begged him to give his earings and armour; Karna who was known for his unfailing charity gave away both the desired things.

Indra feeling quite happy and satisfied then asked Karna to ask for any boon; and Karna asked Indra to give his divine weapon 'Sakthi' which could kill enemies with its power.

Indra granted the boon but on one condition. He said:

"You can use this only once."

So also he received earlier the curse of Parasurama for telling a lie and deceiving him.

Dronachariar was the son of a Brahmin named Bharadwaja. He studied Vedas and other Hindu scriptures. Then he devoted all his time in pursuing the art of using weapons and archery. He thus became famous in his field.

Drupada was a fellow student of Drona in the same ashram. He was the son of the king of Panchala. They were good friends; both of them were close and intimate; they were so intimate that Drupada used to tell his friend Drono frequently that he would like to give atleast half of his kingdom as and when he gets the throne himself.

Dronachariar at the end of his coaching from Bharadwaja in the hermitage got married to the sister of Kripachariar. The couple gave birth to a son who was Aswathamma. His married life propelled him to acquire wealth for the sake of his wife and son. On learning that Parasurama was giving his riches to Brahmins, he decided to meet him. Quite unfortunately, Parasurama had already given away his wealth, and so he could not help Drona. Parsurama felt very much and as an alternative, he offered voluntarily to teach him the use of weapons effectively.

In the meantime, Drupada had become the king of Panchala when his father died. On learning this news, Drona decided to meet him in order to get some help. When he approached his old friend Drupada, he insulted Drona saying.

"Friendship is possible only between equals; how could you ever think that you could be a friend of a king when you are just a wandering beggar?"

Such a harsh and unfriendly statement from his old friend Drupada was a great shock to Drona. He, however, took a vow to punish his arrogance later at an opportune time. He then decided to go to Hastinapura and to search for employment.

On the way, Drona proved his supreme skill to Yudhishtira and a few princes. Karna and Duryodhana were ordered by Drona to bring Drupada as a captive. But as they failed in their attempts, Arjuna was sent with the same task and he successfully brought Drupada as a captive.

Drona said to Drupada

"King of Panchala! you insulted me saying that a king alone could be a friend to a king. Presently, I am also a king, now that I have conquered your kingdom. Now we are equals."

Drona, who thus taught him a lesson, however, treated him with respect; still Drupada could not forget the insult he had felt from Drona. He took a vow and performed a 'yaaga'/'yagna' for a son who would be capable of killing Drona and for a daughter who would be fortunate enough in marrying Drona's best student Arjuna.

Duryodhana was not in a happy state of mind. That was because of his jealousy and hatred against the popularity of the Pandava brothers. The mighty strength of Bhima and the dexterous skill of Arjuna in the use of bow and arrows had caused a lot of worry in his mind.

Besides, people praised the Pandavas openly. They openly declared that Yudhishtira alone would be fit enough to be the king. They thought Dhrithrashtra could never ascend the throne as he was blind. Bhishma cannot be thought of, as he had already taken a vow. Yudhishtira is the only one who could rule the kingdom in all fairness and justice.

Duryodhana was grief-stricken and bewildered. He went to Dhritarashtra and said:

> "What would be our fate if Yudhishtira is to usurp the throne? We would be like beggars in the street depending on them for everything in life."

Dhrithrashtra agreed by nodding his head:

> "Dear Son! What you say is true, However, I am sure that Yudhishtira will never move away from the path of honesty. People love Pandu for his virtues and nobility. So we can not oppose them easily. People would rise up agsinst us and punish us"

But Duryodhana said:

> "My dear Father! your fears are imaginary and baseless; Bhishma as a saintly and righteous person would always be neutral; Drona, Kripa and Aswathamma will certainly support me.

Vidura will not oppose me openly. So we shall send the Pandavas to Varanavata wherethe religious festival in honour of Lord Siva would take place shortly".

Other members in the kingdom also joined Duryodhana and persuaded the king to do what Duryodhana had wished. Sakuni, Kanika, his minister also approved the plan.

Kanika further said:

"The pandavas are not only popular but they are powerful too! So our enemies should be destroyed at any cost."

Plans were executed successfully and the unsuspecting Pandavas were persuaded to go to Varanavata and they finally moved on to Varanavata. Duryodhana was quite happy. He plotted with Sakuni and Karna to kill Kunti and her sons in Varnavata. Purochana, a trusted minister was called for and secret instructions were given to him.

According to the already – finalised Master Plan, Purochana had built a beautiful place at Varanavata with all kinds of inflammable materials like Jute, lac, ghee, oil and fat. The Minister had already planned to set fire to the wax palace at night when they (Pandava brothers and their mother) were asleep.

At the time of Pandava's departure to Varnavrata, the wise Vidura gave a secret warning to Yudhishtira asking all of them to be careful and cautious about the dangers they might have to face.

Vidura advised:

> *"Dear Yudhishtira! The wise man always uses his intelligence to counteract the dangers he expects from his enemy. The fire that destroys a forest cannot hurt a rat which safely escapes by taking shelter in a hole or a porcupine which burrows in the earth".*

When the Pandavas arrived at Varanavata, the people were very happy and they gave a warm welcome to them. The Pandavas then occupied their places in the magnificent royal mansion. Yudhishtira told all the family members about the intentions of Duryodhana. They were, however, greatly relieved to learn secretly that Vidura had sent an expert miner to dig a tunnel as a secret exit passage for all of them to escape.

In the meantime, they got a secret message that the enemies would do their work in the dark hours of the night. In the early hours of midnight, the Pandavas themselves set fire to the palace and escaped unhurt.

When the blind Dhrithrashtra, Duryodhana and his brothers, their uncle Sakuni and Radheya otherwise known as Karnan heard this news about the fire accident they all felt inwardly quite happy thinking that they were all already dead; but they pretended to be sad to the eyes of the public. They also spent lavishly for the funeral rites.

Vidura though quite happy at heart pretended to be sad. Bhishma was in great grief but Vidura explained to him in secret all that had happened.

* * *

The Meeting of Hidimbi in the Forest

The Pandavas escaped through the deep, dark tunnel and reached the nearby forest. They all lay down under a shady tree. At that time they caught sight of a rakshasi or demoness named Hidimbi. She ruled over the forest.

One day, Bhima went to the nearby river to fetch water. At that time, Hidimbi happened to see him and instantly she fell in love with him. It was almost a love at first sight. She herself made a propsal for marriage to Bhima. At the same time she realized that she as a demoness couldnot marry a human being. That being the situation, Hidimba, her brother also objected to this marriage. Thus there was a fight between Bhima and Hidimba in which Hidimba got defeated and died.

Bhima then took Hidimbi to his mother and with her consent he married Hidimbi who looked after the Pandavas giving them good food and care. Soon, Hidimbi became pregnant and she gave birth to a son called Ghatotkacha.

When Bhima, his mother Kunti and his brother left the forest for the neighbouring city Ekachakra, Hidimbi did not like to accompany them as she did not like to live anywhere with her son other than the forest.

They all left for Ekachakra only on the advice of Vyasar.

* * *

The Episode of Bakasura

At Ekachakra, people especially, the Pandavas lived in the disguise of Brahmins begging for food; they bring home their food. Kunti divided it into two parts one part was only for Bhima and the other part is to be shared by all.

On a particular day, Kunti heard some lamentations from the neighbour's house. It was a woman's cry. Kunti ran to that house and made enquiries about the reasons for her lamentation.

"O dear neighbour! Thank you for your sympathy. I really wonder how you can help me. This is about a cruel deed being carried out reguarly by a wicked Rakshasa by name Bakasura. Previously the Rakshasa used to pounce upon people. He would kill them cruelly and eat their flesh."

"To put an end to this cruelty, the people of Ekachakra had made an agreement with the giant that they would send a person daily and a cart-load of rice and other eatables. Tomorrow comes my turn and I will have to send my only son to the demon Bakasura; God alone can help me."

Kunti consoled that woman and said:-

"Please don't worry, I shall send my son Bhima in the place of your son".

Accordingly, the next day, Bhima drove the cart to the giant's cave. Bhima, being a great glutton could not resist his hunger. He ate all the food intended for the giant and emptied the vessel. When the demon came out of the cave, he was utterly disappointed. The giant ran towards Bhima to eat him. There was a fierce fight between Bhima and Bakasura. At last Bhima pushed the demon down and smashed him to death.

* * *

The Swayamvaram of Draupadi

The king of Panchala was Drupada. He had a brother named Dhrishtadyumna. Drupada had a great admiration for Arjuna as he was a great warrior. He thought that such a good warrior as Arjuna would be the suitable match for his daughter Draupadi.

Although Drupada thought that the Pandavas were all dead, he had also heard rumours that the Pandavas were still alive. So he hoped that Arjuna would certainly attend the Swayamvaram.

Draupada made all arrangements for conducting the Swayamvaram at a city called Kampilaya. People were happy and eager to witness the colourful ceremony. The whole city wore a festive look.

At the centre of the Swayamvaram hall, a raised, circular shaped stage (platform /dais) was erected where at the centre a huge vessel of water was placed. There was a revolving disc right above the vessel with a fish hooked to it. A bow and five arrows were placed nearby. Any aspiring contestant to marry Draupadi would have to string the bow and shoot the arrows in quick succession and hit the eye of the fish. One valid and important condition is that the contestant should do it only by looking at its reflection on the surface of the water kept below.

Fig 2: Swyayamwar of Panchala's Princess–

Fig 3: Arjuna Shooting at the fish

No doubt, it was extremely a difficult test. King Drupada did it with a purpose. He knew very well that only an expert archer like Arjuna could accomplish the deed successfully.

A good number of princes had come there to prove their skill. Duryodhana, Karna, Jarasanda, the king of Magadha, Sisupala, Shalya and many more kings were also there.

A beautiful girl who was no other than Draupadi entered the hall captivating the attention of everybody in the hall. All the aspirants were anxiously waiting for the final result.

"Will I be lucky enough to marry Draupadi? Will she be mine?"

They, all thought.

So many kings and Princes tried their luck. A few were not even able to lift the bow. Then when Karna stood up and moved towards the dais, Draupadi did not permit him saying that she could not marry the son of a charioteer.

Then Arjuna rose up. Impressed by Arjuna's personality added by his noble look, she permitted him to participate in the contest. There were still some objections from the crowd as Arjuna seemed to be a Brahmin youth.

Draupadi, however, captivated by the valiant hero, Arjuna, garlanded him.

Thus Arjuna gained the hand of Draupadi and he with his newly wedded bride entered the house along with Bhima, Yudhishtira, Nakula and Sahadeva.

> *"Yudhishtira in a fit of happiness called out his mother and shouted, "Mother! Come out and look at what alms we have got today".*

Kunti Devi, their mother, as usual, answered from inside:

> *"Better share it equally among yourselves as you have been doing all these days".*

Later on, after a while Kunti Devi realized her mistake; she felt sorry and was very sad over the blunder she had committed.

> *"O! God! What a blunder I have committed, I thought it was the daily alms they have brought. That's why I said, Better have it all yourselves together,"*

Said Kunti Devi.

> *"O! Mother! Please do not worry about your statement; your words would never become untrue. Be assured that all the brothers – five of us would marry Panchali".*

So saying all the Five Pandavas garlanded her and accepted her as their wife.

She then welcomed Draupadi warmly, It was then Krishna and his brother Balarama arrived there. Kunti Devi was elated, to see her nephews, she as the sister of their father Vasudeva and also her five sons, the so-called Pandavas.

* * *

The Rajasuya Yagna

It was a long-felt desire of Yudhishtira to create a beautiful place called Indraprastha. That was the time, Maya, the architect of the Asuras voluntarily came forward to help Yudhishtira. Krishna agreed to this proposal and asked him to build a magnificent sabha at Indraprastha. Maya's ambition is to have this sabha built as an impressive competitive one and equivalent to Indra's sabha.

Dhrithrashtra could not tolerate the fame and name, popularity and prosperity of the Pandavas. He had totally forgotten that they were the children of his own brother. His hatred against the Pandavas grew more and more day by day; Circumstances also developed in such a way that he had to necessarily give away half the kingdom to the Pandavas. As he had no interest in this task, he deliberately gave them a barren and uncultivable land.

In spite of this drawback, Yudhishtira accepted it magnanimously and he with the help of all his brothers, Draupadi and Kunti turned the whole place into a great city with all amenities. This place was made the glorious place called Indraprastha.

Gradually Yudhishtira earned the praise of all the people as well as the neighbouring kings who sought his help. They paid even monetary gifts. His coffers easily got filled with gifts. Soon he wanted to expand his kingdom.

That was the time, many of his good friends who were also his well-wishers advised him to conduct a Rajasuya Yagna which would pave a path to him for becoming an Emperor of a vast kingdom. Though Yudhishtira was impressed with this good suggestion, he had his own hesitation in doing so. He had doubts whether there could be any king who would oppose him.

* * *

The Episode of Jarasandha

So he sought the advice of Krishna. Krishna told him that Jarasandha, the king of Magadha would be the only one who would probably oppose him. So he said that Jarasandha must be defeated first. Jarasandha was both wicked and undesirable. He had threatened many kings. But Yudhishtira was yet hesitant.

After a deep discussion with Krishna and other brothers, they came to the conclusion that they must first go to Jarasanda's capital Girivraja. It was also decided that they must all go in disguise.

It was Jarasandha who was born strongly with a body made up of two halves. There was a lady by name Jara who was able to join the two parts with her divine powers thus enabling the whole body become a baby. She also blessed the baby with great power.

The Pandavas and Krishna came in their disguise as Brahmins in order to participate in the yagna. Jarasandha being a great warrior could notice some scars on their faces. He understood that they must be war-torn scars. In that large crowed, he could notice the presence of Bhima by identifying him correctly. He learned from them that they had come over there only to have a fight with him. In that combat, both of them i.e. Jarasandha and Bhima proved to be good fighters. No doubt, the one was very much equal to the other. At the end, Bhima could throw him down and split Jarasandha's body into two halves. But the strange happening was that the two halves of the body joined together immediately. Jarasandha also stood up and began to fight.

Bhima was bewildered and perplexed. He did not know what to do. He looked at Krishna for proper guidance at that critical moment. Krishna took a straw on his hand, tore it into two halves and finally threw the two half pieces in completely opposite directions. Bhima luckily could understand Krishna's gestures from the hint. He then immediately tore him into two pieces and threw them far away from each other in two opposite directions. The two pieces could not come back together and thus Jarasandha died.

Then all those who were imprisoned by Jarasandha were freed by the Pandavas and Jarasandha's son was crowned as the king of Magadha. Then Yudhishtira proclaimed himself as the emperor of many regions around.

Yudhishtira then made all elaborate arrangements for the Rajasuya Yagna and invited many kings. He also extended his invitation to Duryodrana, Karna, Drona, Bhishma,

Sakuni, the king of Gandhara, Krishna, his relative Sisupala who all responded to his invitation and attended the grand ceremony.

It was a traditional custom in those days to honour an important and worthy guest in the whole gathering on the final day. Yudhishtira was to be proclaimed as the great Emperor. Yudhishtira decided to honour Krishna as he was the most worthy man amongst the guests.

* * *

The Episode of Sisupala

Sisupala was the king of Chedi. Somehow he had hatred against Krishna for quite a long time. So, he insulted Krishna calling him names such as - son of a cowherd, thief etc.

Bhishma the grand old man could not relish this. He addressed the crowd and revealed the secret behind his birth. Sisupala was born with an ugly appearance; added to this, he had three eyes and four arms. There was already a prediction made by astrologers that he would die at the hands of the person who would remove his ugliness by some cure. His mother searched for someone who would cure him of his ugliness. At last she took this ugly child to Dwaraka and by his sacred touch, Krishna cured the child. She felt sad about the astrological predictions. But Krishna consoled the mother and said:

> *"Dear aunt! For your sake, I can excuse even about one hundred mistakes of Sisupala but if he exceeds his limit, there is no other way for him but to die".*

But Sisupala did not change his attitude. He continued to heap insults on Bhishma and Krishna. When Krishna could not tolerate further, he chopped his head using his Sudarshana Chakra.

Rajasuya Yagna was thus conducted with all pomp and glory. Yudhishtira assumed the title of "Emperor". All the dignified visitors praised Yudhishtira for the excellent yagna performed on a grand scale.

The celebrations were slightly made unpleasant by only one incident. That is Sisupala's untruly behaviour.

But Duryodhana could not tolerate the success and prosperity of Pandavas. His Jealousy increased when he saw Yudhishtira's magnificent palace so beautifully and artistically designed and built. It was not easy for anyone to differentiate between a fountain of water and the radiant crystal floor. His hatred and jealousy grew so much that he lost his balance. In his fit of anger, by mistaking for the floor, he slipped into water and fell down. Draupadi who happened to witness this scene from the balcony burst into laughter uncontrollably. He thought that this was an insult and got infuriated.

His mind grew wild and he inwardly planned to punish the Pandavas by driving them out of Indraprastha at any cost.

The sage Vyasar appreciated Yudhishtira for having earned the title of 'Emperor' and blessed him with his sweet words. But he also warned him saying that he, however, would have to undergo sorrow and suffering for the ensuing thirteen years. The sage, further, said:

"No one can avoid the effects of destiny. Do perform good deeds. Be always righteous; be vigilant in ruling over the kingdom."

Yudhishtira was grief-stricken about his future.

Arjuna consoled him and said,

"As an Emperor, you should not lose courage. Have a good strength of mind and face destiny boldly."

Duryodhana was torn with jealousy seeing the prosperity of Yudhishtira. Sakuni, his uncle asked him:

"Why are you so sad and gloomy? What has made you sorrowful?"

Duryodhana explained to Sakuni the reasons for his grief. Duryodhana also said:

"Uncle, I have the support of many kings. Why not we wage a war against Duryodhana and drive him out of Indraprastha?"

Sakuni Said:

"Your Plan to defeat Yudhishtira in a war won't be as easy as you think. My dear nephew, I have a plan by which Yudhishtira would be driven out of Indraprastha without a war or shedding of blood".

"Uncle is it possible to do that without shedding of anybody's blood?"

Sakuni Said:

"O! Yes. I have a grand plan. You know Yudhishtira is fond of the game of dice; but he is not skilful in the game, he is also ignorant of several tricks in the game. I know the tricks of the game and let me play on your behalf. He would almost be a child of helplessness. I could easily defeat him in the game and win his kingdom and all his wealth for you!"

* * *

The Invitation of Dhrithrashtra to Yudhishtira for a Game of Dice

Duryodhna, his uncle Sakuni met Dhrithrashtra and explained to him their intentions to invite Duryodhana for playing a game of dice. At first Dhrithrashtra was hesitant to give his consent to their plan. He even addressed his son Duryodhana saying:

> *"My son! Do not develop any hatred towards the Pandavas. We will be losers if we do so; you should not be jealous of your brother, you are also as heroic as your brother. I do not think it wise to antagonize them".*

But Duryodhana was very adamant. So he said that he had grown old and to he could do as he liked. Finally Vidura was deputed to go to Yudhishtira and invite him on Duryodhana's behalf to come and play dice.

* * *

Vidura's Mission to Yudhishtira

Yudhishtira was surprised to see Vidura. His face was sad and desolate. He, however, made inquiries:

> *"Vidhura! How about Hastinapura? Are they all doing well?"*

Vidhura Said:

> *"Everybody in Hastinapura is doing well. King* **Dhrithrashtra** *has built a new hall of games. The king has sent me here to invite you and your brothers on his behalf to come and see the hall and to play a game of dice".*

Yudhishtira asked Vidura about his advice to which Vidura said:

> *"Everybody will agree that playing the game of dice is not only bad but it is the root of many evils".*

One may naturally wonder how an upright and righteous person like Yudhishtira could respond to this invitation. There are a few reasons that could be attributed to this. Evil things like drinking, lust and gambling would prompt a person if he is fond of anyone of them. Etiquette and good manners amongst the Kshatriyas would never dishonour an invitation. Sage Vyasar had already once warned him about the bickerings and quarrels between the two families that might lead to the destruction of the whole race.

That's why Yudhishtira was careful in accepting the invitation.

Yudhishtira, his brothers, his mother and all other helpers arrived at Hastinapura and stayed for the night in the allotted place.

Next morning all the people gathered in the hall. Sakuni announced all details about the game and made all arrangements for starting the game.

Fig 4: Sakuni is the master of dice game

The game was about to commence. When Yudhishtira was hesitant for a while, he was ridiculed by Sakuni saying.

"If you are afraid of playing and are very much attached to your wealth, you need not play, But do not tell lame excuses".

Yudhishtira felt shy and said,

"All right! Who is to play the game with me, first?"

Duryodhana said:

"Let us begin the game with stakes first in the form of wealth and precious gems. My uncle Sakuni will play on my behalf and cast the dice".

It was a terrible shock to Yudhishtira; with great hesitation, he said,

"When you have invited me to play the game, how could Sakuni play on your behalf?"

Duryodhana laughed and said:

"Are you afraid of losing to my uncle?"

Yudhishtira felt shy and replied

"I am not a coward, all right I shall play"

The great assembly was full. Many onlookers including Bheeshma, Vidura, Drona, Kripa, Dhrithrashtra, his family members, Karnan and Aswathamma were all there.

At first gold, silver and ornaments were the stakes and Yudhishtira lost them in no time. Next he pledged his servants, his chariots, horses, armies and lost them. His brothers made a plea to stop the game which fell on his deaf ears. Then he staked Nakula and Sahadeva followed by Bhima and Arjuna. He lost them too!

It was then Sakuni who told him that he had one more precious jewel. He could very well stake that too and that was his wife Draupadi. He did so and lost his wife Draupadi too!

The whole gathering was stunned. A few of them wept in distress. Bhishma, Drona and Kripa were all worried.

When Vidura was asked to fetch Draupadi, he refused. Then a charioteer by name Pratikami was ordered to do. Duryodhana's prime intention was to humiliate her openly in the presence of all in the gathering. But she refused to go to the place of Duryodhana. She protested and argued:

> "How could anybody stake his wife when he had himself lost the game? How could he pledge me when he had himself lost all his freedom and thereby lost all rights". I refuse to go to the place of Duryodhana?"

When this message was brought by the charioteer-messenger, Duryodhana got wild and shouted with anger. He called Duhsasana and said:

"My brother, Duhsasana! Go and fetch that woman here, Drag her by the hair.

Duhsasana being the brother of Duryodhana who was also as wicked and villainous as Duryodhana hurried to the place of Draupadi, dragged her by her hair and reached the hall where all have gathered.

"Duhsasana, why should this slave need dress?; remove her dresses and hand them over to uncle Sakuni" shouted Karna.

Draupadi wept and cryingly appealed to everybody in the court hall including elders like Bhishma, Dronachariar, Karna and Dhrithrashtra. But Duryodhana ignored the advice of all the elderly people and asked Duhasasana to seize her garments and disrobe her. The whole gathering was trembled with fear not knowing what to do at this juncture. They were all helpless and Draupadi was grief-stricken and cried for help. She could only appeal to Gods and prayed to Lord Krishna for help.

Fig 5: Draupadi's Vastraharan

When Duryodhana tried to pull her sari, so many saris, one after another would fall on her body and cover up. (conceal her body) and soon a heap of sarees got piled up in the hall.

It was nothing but a miracle. It was God's intervention and a mighty help to the suffering victim, Draupadi.

After sometime when Draupadi slowly opened her eyes, the Pandavas were standing in one corner. They were all ashamed of themselves and were bending their heads down in utter shame. The whole place was engulfed in silence.

Of all the persons, it was only Bhima who broke the silence. He instantly took a pledge and swore.

> *"Sooner or later, I shall pierce his thigh tear his heart out and drink the blood of Duhasasana for the sinful deed he has committed at this Assembly"*

> *Arjuna also shouted in anger and informed the whole assembly swearing "I pledge and take a vow that I shall certainly kill Karna for having insulted and humiliated Draupadi".*

> *Next Sahadevan said firmly," I shall undoubtedly kill Sakuni".*

> *Nakula swore and said, "It is certain that I will kill Sakuni's son and all those wicked people who kept quiet silently seeing this unbearable deed".*

Panchali Sabatham (Vow):

Draupadi also took a pledge and swore saying:

> *"I will not tie up my hair till Duhsasana is killed and till my hair is dipped in Duhsasana's blood".*

This is known as the oft-quoted **'Panchali Sabatham'** (**Vow**):

Even Nature seemed to be upset over this sad happening. Suddenly the earth began to quiver; There were so many other evil omens. There was thunder and storm; rain also began to pour. It looked as if that all these sudden happenings were the sight of Nature's fury!

Dhrithrashtra was also upset over the incidents that took place in the hall. He also felt guilty and so he called Draupadi and tried to comfort her saying:

> *"My Child, No doubt, my son has committed a great sin. I shall give you whatever you want as an* ***atonement*** *for all his mistakes".*

Draupadi being a devout wife said:

> *"Great Lord! I need only two favours from you. Let my husbands be freed from bondage. Secondly let me appeal to you for the return of all our weapons".*

It was a sudden turn of events. This, perhaps, prompted the Pandavas to leave that place. Draupadi also followed them.

Duryodhana was not happy with his father's actions. He was rather angry that his blind father had freed the Pandavas from bondage.

He wanted his father Dhrithrashtra again to call Yudhishtira for playing a game of dice. He also laid down some conditions for the game of dice, i.e. whoever loses the game, he must go on exile to the forest for twelve years and spend the thirteenth year without being seen by others. In case, they were to be recognized during the thirteenth year, they were to go into exile for another twelve years.

Human nature is such that Yudhishtira could not say 'no' to his uncle Dhritarashtra and also he could not resist the temptation. So, finally he played the game and lost it too!

In accordance with the rules of the game, he set out for the forest.

Krishna learned about this and so he went to Hastinapura. From there he took his sister Subadra, wife of Arjun and her young son Abhimanya to Dwaraka.

When Draupadi's brother Dhristadyumna heard about all these untoward incidents, he felt so much that he took a vow to revenge against the Kauravs. Vidura took Kunti to his place.

* * *

Pandava's Exile into the Forest

As righteous persons who always follow the path of Dharma, the Pandavas set out for the forest called Kamyaka in agreement with the stipulated conditions. When they all started moving, People cried and lamented by crowding the streets.

The blind king Dhrithrashtra, though was the cause of all these developments, yet he was upset over the incidents. He also felt guilty inwardly. So he wanted to know the pulse of the people, how they received all these turn of events and how they felt about it.

He therefore sent for Vidura and wanted to know -what the citizens had said. Vidura answered saying that their leaders had left them.

> *"They cursed you, all the entire Kuru race who have caused such bad things to happen".*

When Dhrithrashtra and Vidura were thus discussing, the sage Narada appeared before them suddenly and announced.

"In fourteen years from henceforth (today), the Kaurva race will become extinct as a result of the sins committed by Duryodhana".

Duryodhana and his friends were shaken with fear and sought advice from Dronachariar. Drona said that for all the sinful deeds that they had committed, Nemesis will overtake them at the end of the fourteenth year.

Life for Yudhishtira, his wife Draupadi and his brothers was very tough in the Kamyaka forest. They all had to undergo many hardships over there. They could not forget the treachery of Duryodhana. So they all decided to move on to another forest and did so.

At the kingdom, Duryodhana was greatly disturbed in mind and worried about the banished Pandavas. At the end of their exile which is nearing its end, the Pandavas won't keep quiet, Duryodhana feared. So he revealed his plan to Karna and Sakuni. This would be the proper time to fight against and to defeat them, he said to Karna and Sakuni.

Duryodhana knew that the elders won't agree to this. So the wicked Duryodhana had a different plan. Under the pretext of counting the cattle in all the forests, they all set out for the forest where the Pandavas were in exile.

At that point of time, Indra, King of the Gods prompted, from high above, Chitrasena, a Gandharva King to intercept and waylay Duryodhana and his army.

He promptly did so and defeated Duryodhana. Then he dragged Duryodhana and brought him before Yudhishtira. But he, being a highly good-natured man who always followed the path of Dharma, did not punish Duryodhana but released him freely. Yet, Duryodhana being a wicked man felt insulted and decided to wreak vengeance against Yudhishtra and his brothers.

During their stay in the forest, Pandavas had the chance of meeting many saints and seers. Even in the midst of difficulties they never swerved from the path of Dharma. Bhima could meet Hanuman who was said to be his elder brother. Arjun could do his penance successfully and he was able to get many mighty weapons from Easwar, the very Creator. He could also meet Dharma*, the God of Death and Kubera, the God of wealth. In addition to his skill in archery, he learned from Chitrasena dance and music.

The period of exile for Pandavas was coming to an end and because of their tough life and frequent wanderings, they became weary and tired. Once in the forest a deer while running stopped and rubbed its body against a Brahmin's 'Arani' (a kind of mortar stone for kindling/making fire). While the deer was trying to run back, the stone got entangled in its antlers. The deer was frightened and it tried

---

* 'Yama', the God of Death is always known as Yama Raja Dharma

to shake off the mortar stone but in vain. Then the deer started running fast.

The Brahmin being poor was worried and asked for help from the Pandavas. He required the Arani for his daily prayers. So he wanted the Pandavas to chase the deer and recover his Arani. The Pandavas all in five chased and chased but they could not catch the deer which ran for a long distance and suddenly vanished.

* * *

Pandava's Meeting an Yaksha

As they were running for a long time, they became weary and thirsty. Yudhishtira instructed his younger brother Sahadeva to fetch water from any lake nearby.

Sahadeva who had gone to the nearby lake was not to be seen even after a long time. Yudhishtira got worried and sent Nakula in search of Sahadeva. After some reasonable time Bhima was sent. He was followed by Arjun. Atlast Yudhishtira himself started. After covering some distance, he saw a lake where the water was clear. So, he thought that all his brothers should be there somewhere around the lake.

When he went near the lake, he found, to his shock, all his brothers were lying dead. It was a mystery to Yudhishtira who was almost in tears.

"What had happened?"

He asked himself.

The brothers, four in number excepting Yudhishtira had gone one after another to fetch water from the lake. There was an Yaksha who prevented them from taking water from the lake before answering his questions. He said they could take water after answering his questions.

The word Yaksha denotes a demi-God and its race serving Kubera, the God of wealth. This Yaksha serving the Lord of Dharma had appeared to test Yudhishtira.

So the Yaksha asked him whether he could answer his questions and if only he answered he could very well take water from the lake.

"Are you ready to answer my questions?"

Asked the Yaksha.

Yudhishtira very calmly said:

"You can very well ask me anything you like. I shall try to answer to the best of my knowledge."

"What is that which has the fastest speed?"

"Speed of the mind".

"What makes sun shine every day?"

"The Power of Brahman"

"What do you need to face danger?"

"Courage"

"What is nobler than the earth?"

"Mother".

"Who is the friend of a man at home?"

"The wife".

"Who accompanies a man in death?"

"Dharma"

"What is happiness?"

"Good Conduct gives one happiness".

"What makes one a real brahmana? Is it birth, good conduct or learning?"

"It is not birth or learning, Good conduct only; learning without good conduct does not make a real brahmana".

"Which is the greatest wonder in the world?"

"Everyday we see a good number of people die. Yet, Man thinks he is permanent. This is the greatest wonder in the world".

The Yaksha thus posed many questions and Yudhishtira answered them all. The Yaksha was pleased.

At the end, the Yaksha asked:

"I can give back life to one of your brothers. To whom would you give priority?

Although Yudhishtira loved all his brothers,

"My brother, Nakula".

He unhesitatingly said.

The Yaksha was surprised:

> *"When there are Bhima and Arjun why do you choose Nakula?"*

Yudhishtira quite calmly said:

> *"Sir, I do agree with you. It's true that Bhima and Arjun are my brothers Nakula is my step mother's son. How can I sacrifice him for the sake of my own brothers?*

In appreciation of Yudhishtira's broad outlook, the Yaksha revived Nakula from lifelessness.

> *"I can give back life to another brother. This time whom do you prefer?"*

asked the Yaksha.

"Sahadeva,"

Yudhishtira said.

The Yaksha was surprised.

> *"This time atleast, you could have asked for life to one of your valiant brothers".*

> *"Sir! When my father died, My mother Madri also died. She asked me to treat Nakula and Sahadeva as my own brothers. How would I change my mind?"*

Said Yudhishtira.

The Yaksha was highly pleased with Yudhishtira for his impartiality and uprightness. He revived Bhima and Arjun. Then he blessed all of them.

The Yaksha was no other than the God of Death, Yama, father of Yudhishtira. He addressed his son with love and affection and said:

> *"Dear Yudhishtira, your exile is almost over. You have to live incognito for one more year. All your hardships, trials and tribulations will be over. My advice is that you can go to king Virata's Matsya Kingdom and live there in disguise".*

The Pandavas then set out for Matsya Kingdom.

On the advice of the Yaksha who was not other than Yama, the God of Death, the Pandavas proceeded to the Kingdom of Matsya. They had already lived in exile in the forest for twelve years. Now they had to live incognito for one more year without revealing their true identity. If by ill-luck, if any one found out, they had to again live in exile in the forest for another period of twelve years. They should spend the thirteenth year of exile carefully undiscovered by anyone especially by the spies of Duryodhana.

So they entered the city of Matsya in disguise. They carefully covered all their weapons in a big gunny bag. They hung it to the branch of a tree outside the city.

Then Yudhishtira gained entry into the court of king, Virata had acquired the King's friendship in his disguise calling himself **Kankabhatta.** After gaining some confidence for himself from king **Virata,** he asked for permission form the king and enlisted himself in service as a courtier. As a Courtier, he would please the king by playing the game of dice with him and delight him with his jokes. With his knowledge of astrology and Vedas he would be able to make some predictions for future guidance.

Bhima said that he would serve as a cook in the court of Virata. As an expert in cooking he would prepare tasty food for the king, he would cut the trees in the forest and bring firewood for the kitchen and finally he would also please the king by conquering the wrestlers in the court. He would call himself **Valala.**

Arjuna said that he would disguise himself as a eunuch and serve the ladies in the court especially teaching the women singing and dancing. As he had already learnt music and dance from Chitrasena, he would dress up like a woman and teach these Fine Arts to the women and children under the name **Brihannala.**

Then Yudhishtira asked Nakula what he would do in the court of the king; Nakula said that he would find pleasure in training and looking after horses under the name **Damagranth.** He preferred to do this because he knew the heart of horses and their usual ailments and cure. He also said that he was good at horse-riding and harnessing the horses and driving them in a chariot.

Sahadeva said that he would tend the cows under the name **Tantripala** and he would guard Virata's cattle against diseases and wild beasts' attack on them.

Draupadi would call herself **Sairandhri** in the queen's Court as a companion and attendant of Sudheshna, Virata's queen. She also said that she would engage herself in light jobs as combing the hair and entertaining the women of the court.

As everybody in the Pandava's group including Draupadi had desired, they all shone well in their occupations doing their work to the satisfaction of their masters.

The Queen Sudheshna had a brother by name Kichaka. He headed the King's army. He was powerful and wielded a lot of influence. But he was wicked and villainous in character.

It was on one of his visits to his sister, in the queen's personal chamber that Kichaka had an opportunity to see Draupadi. He was enchanted by Draupadi's beauty. He lost himself for a while as he was infatuated by her beauty. He wanted to have her for himself so that he could marry her and live with her happily.

From his sister Sudheshna, he learned that she was a new maid in the queen's chamber and her job is to be an attendant and companion to herself the queen.

As Kichaka was deeply in love with the beautiful Draupadi he sought the help of his sister Queen Sudheshna. She told him pleasingly that it was not at all possible to do so, as she was already married to her five husbands and they would kill Kickaka if they knew this.

But Kichaka insisted on his sister's help in fulfilling his desire. One day, Kichaka arranged for a grand feast in his palace. Queen Sudheshna, out of pity for her brother, thought that she could help him at this favourable time. She therefore called Draupadi and asked her:

> "O! Draupadi! Take this jug of introxicating drink to Kichaka".

Draupadi was hesitant to go to Kichaka's palace as she was afraid of him.

So, she in a humble voice appealed to the queen and said:

> "O! Queen Sudheshna! Please forgive me as I am terribly scared. If you do not mistake me, can't you send somebody else?".

The Queen made a pretence and showed her false anger.

> "No, Daupadi, you must go; why do you get scared? Nothing will happen to you".

With great reluctance in her mind, Draudipadi obeyed the queen and went to Kichaka's palace.

She dropped the jug and fled immediately. The wicked Kichaka chased here and tried to grab her. But Sairandhri ran into the court of king **Virata**. Bhima who was present in the court at that time could understand what could have taken place.

Later Sairandhri met Bhima and wept before him also saying that she would put an end to her life. It was then Bhima realized the gravity and agony of Sairandhri. He assured her saying that he would kill Kichaka.

Next day, when Sairandhri met Kichaka, she told him with all enticing words that she was just scared about her husbands. Secretly in a feeble voice she told him that she had a plan.

> *"Listen! I have a secret plan. Come to the dancing hall late at night".*

This is the plot that both Sairandhri and Bhima contrived. That's why she had asked Kichaka to come to the dancing hall during the night hours secretly.

As already planned Bhima went to the Lady's Chamber in advance and laid himself on the bed and covered himself; when Kichaka came to the room silently, he noticed someone lying on the cot with a sari covered from toe to head. Kichaka then laid his hands on that body thinking that it should be

Sairandhri's. Bhima instantly jumped over Kichaka, thrashed him and killed him. Then he quietly slipped from that place and went and slept on the kitchen floor.

The news of Kichaka's death spread like wild fire everywhere. Although the queen Sudeshna knew who the culprit was, she had no evidence. The mysterious death of Kichaka made Duryodhana have so many doubts and surmises. As a wicked-minded warrior, Duryodhana could guess beyond doubt that only a person like Bhima could have killed a strong and formidable fighter like Kichaka. In addition, he had learnt that the queen Sudeshna's newly-appointed maid Sairandhri had five gandharvaras as her husbands. All these news confirmed the fact that the Pandavas were in the kingdom of Matsya.

The death of Kichaka was the cause of people's anger against Draupadi. The people thought that she would be a dangerous person. So the people suggested that she should be expelled immediately.

Draupadi, however, appealed to the queen asking permission for her to live incognito just for one more month. Draupadi had only one more month to complete this exile without being recognized by anyone. Sudheshna out of pity granted her request.

Duryodhana thought that Kichaka's death would be a terrible blow to King Virata. It would also weaken his strength and courage. So, that would be the proper time for him to attack Virata. The Pandavas also who were living 'incognito' would certainly come out to help king Virata.

Besides, King Susarma, the ruler of Trigarta would also support him and help him in the fight against Virata as the king of Matsya was his direct enemy.

The king, Virata got annoyed and consulted Kanka who was no other than Yudhishtira. He consoled the king and said,

> "O King! Do not worry. Though an hermit, I am; I am known as an expert in warfare I shall wear my armour, go in a chariot and chase the enemies. Order your cook Valala, your stable-keeper Dharmagranthi and your cowherd Tantripala also to take their chariots and help us".

The king, Virata was happy and accepted the offer of Kanka. (the assumed name of Yudhishtira at the court of Virata). The chariots were got ready. King Virata's army under the guidance and leadership of Kanka set out to oppose Susarma. Both sides were equal in their skill yet, Susarma defeated Virata and kept him in his chariot. The capture of Virata dampened the spirit of Virata's army. But the wise Yudhishtira suddenly ordered Bhima to attack Susarma and release king Virata. Bhima ably rallied the scattered Matsya forces, captured Susarma and defeated the army of Susarma.

The people were happy over the victory and they were all getting ready to welcome happily their king Virata.

That was the time, the army of Duryodhana invaded the northern side and tried to steal the herds of cattle.

The affected cowherds appealed to the prince Uttara and requested him to recover the cows. Uttara was ready to help but only required an able charioteer.

The Princes ran to Brihannala (who was no other than Arjuna in the disguise of a woman) asked for his services as a charioteer.

Then Arjuna took him to the tree where the Pandava brothers had hidden their weapons.

> *"O! Uttar, please bring down the weapons from the tree. They are the weapons which belonged to the Pandavas".*

When he saw the weapons from the tree, he felt a little confident and could realize that Brihannalla was really a good warrior. Brihannalla also told Uttara that she was Arjuna. Uttara felt sorry and guilty that he had, by mistake, engaged a great warrior, as a charioteer. Uttara in a humble way and with all reverence said:

> *"Please pardon me, Arjuna for having engaged you, a great archer and warrior as a charioteer, I have committed these blunders because of my ignorance".*

But Arjuna said that he need not worry about him and encouraged him saying that their first and foremost duty was to go and fight in the battlefield.

Arjuna was not an ordinary man but a great soul. As a strong man he thought it was his duty to see that even the cowards rise above their weeknesses. That's why he encouraged him often and tried to put courage into Uttara. This shows Arjuna's nobility. He never abused his strength. He was fittingly called also **Bibhatsu, which means one who shrank from doing any unworthy act and he lived upto it till the last.**

When Duryodhana noticed from a distance Uttarkumar coming in a chariot driven by a female charioteer, he thought that he could win over them easily. That was only a mistaken calculation.

On the other side, Arjuna could notice from a distance the presence of Bhishma, Drona and Kripachariar standing in a row along with Duryodhana and Karna. Arjuna started using his bow and arrow, three arrows one after another fell at the feet of Bhishma, Drona and Kripachariar's feet. This event made everyone shout, "O!, Arjuna is seen here"!

Immediately Duryodhana said in a loud voice:

"Arjuna's identity is revealed before the exile period is over. So the Pandavas should again be in exile for twelve more years".

The learned Acharya Dronachariar retorted saying that the stipulated exile period for the Pandavas was already over.

Uttarkumar under the leadership of Arjuna fought bravely and routed the Kaurava army. Virata was happy to learn about their victory.

It was because of Arjuna, Virata's son got the victory against the Kauravas but virata thought that his son was responsible for the victory. So he was proud of his son and praised him. So Yudhishtira thought that it was high time that he revealed the truth and therefore Yudhishtira said that Brihannala was the person who fought bravely and won the war. Virata did not relish this; Virata did not like the comparison made by Kanka between Uttara and a woman charioteer. So in his sudden anger, the king Virata threw the dice he was playing on the face of Kanka. He also gave him a slap on his face. Yudhishtira was hurt and blood started oozing. Sairandhri who was standing nearby wiped the face with the corner of her garment and squeezed the blood into a cup.

On seeing this, the king grew angry and said:

"Why do you make a lot of fuss over a trivial matter?"

"O king! It is holy man's blood. Even if a drop of blood falls on the ground, people of this country will not have rain for a year. Each drop indicates a year of famine. You may not know the spiritual greatness of this person. You might also be killed by the one who had planned to do this act. So it is with a good intention to save you from being killed, I collect the

blood of such a precious man." – said Sairandhri who was no other than Kunti Devi.

Just then Uttarkumar arrived at the palace; king Virata was surprised to learn from him who really they were. He felt sorry for having treated the royal people as servants. The Queen also felt very much and she appealed to Draupadi for her pardon.

Virata expressed his gratitude to the Pandavas for having helped him in safeguarding their country. To make atonement for all his faults, he gave his daughter, Princess Uttara in marriage to Abhimanyu, Arjuna's son. The wedding was solemnised in the presence of Krishna, Balaram and Drupada.

The exile period – as a punishment imposed on the Pandavas has been successfully completed by the five brothers and Kunti Devi. A few section of the people wanted the Pandavas to defeat the Kauravas in a battle field. But they also knew the deadly effects of a warfare. Krishna's wish was that the Pandavas should avoid a war. But at the same time he felt that if the Kauravas were not accepting a settlement they should wage a war. Otherwise, it would be misunderstood as cowardice. He also knew very well that Duryodhana would never accept this proposal.

The Pandavas had successfully completed their exile period. They could freely move about revealing their identity as Pandavas. So they settled openly in Upaplavya, a place in

Matsya kingdom. From there they had contacts with friends and relatives.

Balarama, Krishna, Arjuna's wife Subhadra and her son Abhimanyu came from Dwaraka. Many yadava warriors also came along with them.

The wedding celebrations of Abhimanyu with Princess uttara was solemnised in the presence of Krishna and other august gathering of friends and relatives. When the noise of merriment of the wedding celebrations were over, Krishna rose up to speak.

He spoke about the story of Ill-treatment and Ingratitude of Duryodhana towards the Pandavas. Krishna further spoke:

> *"How deceitful he is! Don't you all remember how Duryodhana had cheated Yudhishtira in the game of dice by tricks and deceits? How patiently and decently Yudhishtira had endured all the troubles; yet Yudhishtira never thought of doing any wrong deeds to the sons of Dhritarashtra. He was magnanimons in bearing the fraud and meanness of Kauravas. Now I shall try to send a sincere emissary to persuade Duryodhana to a peaceful settlement by giving back half the kingdom to Yudhishtira".*

Balarama then rose up to talk,

> *"I fully agree with Krishna's suggestion. Nothing would be as good as this plan for both Duryodhana*

and Yudhishtira. The envoy should speak gently and in a friendly way to Bhishma, Dhristarashtra, Drona, Vidura and also Karna and to many others to secure support for the Pandavas. I want the envoy to approach Duryodhana tactfully to make peace with him. Let us try to avoid further conflicts so that no war in a battlefield could be caused."

Satyaki, one of the Yadava warriors was perturbed with the argument of Balarama and stood up in anger and spoke angrily.

"I do not agree with Balarama. His attitude is not worthy enough to do anything for good. It was Kauravas who invited Dharmaputra to play the game of dice. Not only that, the Kauravas with the artful villainy of Sakuni, cheated him many a time. Being just and righteous, Yudhishtira and his brothers kept their word and lived twelve years in exile in the forest and thereafter twelve months lived incognito. To wage a war against such an enemy is not wrong at all. So without delay, we must prepare ourselves for any eventuality"

Drupada appreciated satyaki's firmness in dealing with the enemy, He said:

"No soft words or peaceful attitude towards Duryodhana would bring him to reason. Let us send word immediately to our friendly Kings Salya, Jayatsena, Kekaya and Dhrishtaketu.

At the sametime we must send a fitting and learned envoy to Dhrithrashtra and convey our message to all his supporters"

Drupada completed his arguments; then Krishna rose up and spoke to Drupada thus in the following manner.

"Your valid suggestion is practicable and is in line with the Royal code and conduct. I have equal ties of affection to both Kauravas and Pandavas. Please instruct your emissary to try his best for a peaceful settlement."

Thus the meeting came to an end and Krishna left for Dwaraka with his people after attending princess Uttara's wedding and thereafter the family meeting.

* * *

Krishna's Mission-Krishna as an Emissary to Peace

As a messenger of peace, Krishna decided to take all earnest efforts to establish peace between the two families. At first, he had a long discussion with the Pandavas; Krishna was surprised when even an angry and mighty person like Bhima wanted to have a peaceful settlement.

He said to Krishna:-

> *"The enmity between the two families shall not destroy the whole race. Let us try to have peace!"*

But Draupadi did not concur with the views of Bhima.

She sobbed when she remembered the shameful act of Duryodhana.

Krishna was moved and said:-

> *"Do not worry; The sons of Dhrithrashtra will not listen to words of peace. They will have a big fall and their bodies will be a feast for dogs and other animals."*

Krishna thus comforted her and left for Duryodhana's palace. When Krishna was to be treated to a grand feast in his honour, he refused to accept and said:

"When emissaries like him go on a mission they eat only after their mission is completed successfully. Hence I can not accept your invitation."

Then he learned that Dhrishtarashtra was waiting for Krishna; he straightaway went to the court of great assemblage of kings.

There he addressed the blind king and said:

"Dhrithrashtra, try to do everything possible for a peaceful settlement. Do not bring ruin to your race. As an elderly man as you are, I ask you, is it not your duty to control and restrain your sons?"

Dhrishtarashtra replied saying:-

"I am powerless and I am not to be blamed; my sons, wicked as they are they do not listen to me. May I, therefore request you, Krishna to advise Duryodhana?"

Krishna then spoke to Duryodhana:-

"Being the descendent of a noble race why don't you pursue the path of Dharma? If you choose to do justice, the Pandavas would enthrone Dhrishtarashtra as king and yo as the heir-apparent; you may honourably nake peace with them by giving them half the kingdom. If not half the kingdom, atleast five villages might be accepted by the Pandavas"

To this Duryodhana firmly said:-

"I will not give the Pandavas, an inch of land, not even a needle point of it"

Duhsasana the brother of Duryodhana, Sakuni, the uncle of Kaurava brothers and Radheya alias Karna, bosom friend of Duryodhana – all of them discussed with Duryodhana as to how they could tackle the situation in which they are forced to accept a peaceful settlement. This kind of peace-proposal was not to be accepted, they thought. Duryodhana therefore ordered his brother Duhsasana to seize Krishna with ropes. Saying so, all of them rushed to Krishna to imprison him.

Human mortals and ordinary humans as they were, they failed to understand that it was impossible to tie down the Great Protector of the universe and Omnipotent Krishna.

* * *

Krishna's Viswarupa

Instantly, Krishna who had anticipated all these laughed fiercely and disclosed his divinity. He thus laughed again when his face shone with radiance All the Devas came out of his body The creator, Brahma, eleven Rudras, the Lords of the four quarters. Indra, Varuna, Kubera and Yama were to be seen glowing with radiance.

The many arms of Krishna were seen holding all the divine weapons; Krishna's famous conch named Panchajanya, the chakra known as Sudarshana, the Gada called Kaumodaki and the sword called Nandaki. Fire flamed out of his eyes and ears. The appearance was strange and terrible. Thus Krishna revealed his Visvarupa which was the magnificent revelation of the supreme Omnipotent. There was a bright and an ever-glowing radiance everywhere.

Everyone was astonished, rather frightfully stupefied with awe and wonder. It was only the foolish Duryodhana and his companions thought that it was a magic trick of Krishna.

The blind Dhrithrashtra temporaraily regained his sight and was able to gaze at the Viswarupa of Krishna. The blind king said to Krishna:

> *"Blessed I am to see your Viswarupa. I wish to see nothing else, could I become blind once again Krishna?"*

And he became blind again as he wished

> *"All our efforts have become futile; Duryodhana is adamant and obstinate"*

said the blind Dhritarashtra to Krishna.

Krishna then went straight to Kunti and narrated all that had happened.

The time has come

War has become inevitable.

Love, Attachment and Duty are our cardinal principless.

When Kunti learnt that the war was inevitable and also a certainty, her mind was tormented by two conflicting thoughts: one was the prospect of losing many lives and thereby a total destruction in a war which she wanted to avoid; And the other one was that as a person belonging to kshatriya race, it was a 'must' that she should uphold the honour of her race; so naturally she and her sons should not withdraw from a war as that would be a dishonour and stigma to the family.

With this agitated mind, she reflected herself and thought,

> *"Will it be possible for my sons to defeat the mighty three warriors combined-Bhishma, Drona and Karna? The grandshire, Bhishma will not certainly want to kill them. Dronachariar too would try to avoid killing my sons because of his love for his own disciples.*
>
> *But Karna would be Pandava's chief enemy. Besides Karna is a great warrior. He would try to kill the Pandavas as that would please his bosom friend Duryodhana who had made him a ruler of a kingdom, "*

In such a situation, she decided to meet Karna and tell him about the secret of his birth. She had the fond hope that once he learnt the truth, he would not fight against his own brothers. Krishna also approved saying that it would be a good idea.

So she went to the bank of the Ganga where Karna usually offers his prayers to the Sun – God every morning. When he finished his prayers, he looked around and found Kunti. He was a little confused and amazed to see her over there.

Karna addressed her respectfully and said:

> *"O! Queen? Being the son of Radha and the chariot – driver Adhiratha, I bow unto you! Can I do anything for you?"*

Kuntidevi said:

> *"Karna! my dear son! you are not the son of the chartioteer; nor Radha is your mother. You are actually the son of Sun-God, Surya. You were born out of the womb of Pritha who comes of royal blood otherwise called Kunti; surprisingly you were born with armour and golden ear-rings."*

She continued and explained

> *"Unfortunately Destiny is such that you do not know that the Pandavas are your brothers. As you have fallen on the side of Duryodhana, you hate your own brothers, not knowing who they actually are!*
>
> *May I therefore suggest that you may join Arjuna to put down the wicked Duryodhana?"*

Karna was agitated and tormented by two conflicting forces whether to join Arjuna and together punish the wicked or to be loyal to Duryodhana and Dhrithrashtra's sons whose salt he had eaten.

> *"Could there be greater treachery or meaner ingratitude?"*

He thought and said with sadness but with firmness:

> *"Mother! You say that my joining the Kauravas would be contrary to the principles of Dharma."*
>
> *"I have eaten the salt of Dhrithrashtra's sons. How can I forsake them now? Mother, should I not pay back my debt? So there is no alternative*

other than using all my powers against your sons.
How could I betray my friend Duryodhana?"

Then, Kunti specifically requested Karna not to kill Arjuna and not to use Nagastra more than once on Arjuna. Karna agreed to this and said to Kunti:

> *"Mother! Please pardon me. In response to your*
> *request, I could only promise and assure you that I*
> *will not fight against Yudhishtira, Bhima, Nakula*
> *or Sahadev. But in the case of Arjuna, I will not*
> *spare him.*
>
> *"Even if Arjuna were to be killed by me at the*
> *battlefield, you would still have five sons. Why do*
> *you get worried much?"*

Kunti went back to her palace with a heavy heart and with mixed feelings.

This is how Destiny played its role!

* * *

The Pandavas Choosing a General for Their Army

Krishna came to Upaplavya where the Pandavas were anxiously waiting. He explained in detail how the adamant and foolish Duryodhana refused to accept a peace-settlement in spite of Gandari's advice.

He added that the circumstances were such that they had to necessarily prepare for a war. He beautifully described that Kurukshetra was waiting for the holocaust.

Now they had to make elaborate preparations for organizing the troops. The marching of any army involves destruction on both sides until the attainment of victory for one of the sides. An army must be divided into several divisions for an effective fighting from all directions.

Orders were issued by Yudhishtira for forming the troops in seven divisions. The chosen heads of these seven divisions were Drupada, Virata, Dhrishtadyumna, Sikandin, Satyaki, Chekitana and Bhimasena.

Then they must choose and appoint a Supreme General from one of these seven for the whole army of seven Divisions.

Sahadeva suggested Virata. Nakula said that Draupada, the father of Draupadi would be fit enough in point of age, wisdom, courage, birth and strength. Next, it was Arjuna who named Dhrishtadyumna to be the chief of the army. He was famous for his skill in archery and even surprised Parasurama. He alone would be the one who could witstand the arrows of Bhishma. Bhimasena uttered the name of Sikhandin who was born to kill Bhishma and he was sure that nobody else could defeat Bhishma.

Then Yudhishtira asked Krishna for his opinion. Krishna said that each one of the names suggested was worthy of selection. He further said that he preferred to endorse Arjuna's choice namely Dhristadyumna, son of Drupada who led Draupadi at the Swayamvara. This was finally accepted by one and all. The roaring noise of the warriors, the blowing of conches and shells and the trumpeting of elephants were heard fiercely in the battlefield at Kurakshetra. And finally the Pandavas' army entered the battlefield in martial uniform.

* * *

Choosing the General for their Army, by the Kauravas

With the acceptance and approval of Duryodhana, Bhishma would lead the troops on the side of Kauravas. Duryodhana respectfully and reverently addressed Bhishma and said:

> *"Our most workshipul leader of our troops!*
>
> *Please lead us with all your might and skill to achieve victory. We will follow you as lovingly as calves follow the mother-like bull"*

Bhishma replied:-

> *"Let it be so! I shall be pleased to lead our troops and discharge my duties sincerely. I might be killing so many in the battle-field but I can not kill the sons of Pandu.*
>
> *One more thing, Karna, the son of Surya whom you respect is opposed to my leadership from the beginning. You might very well give him the leadership of the army. I wouldn't object to it"*

Karna then addressed Duryodhana and said:-

> *"As long as Bhishma is alive, I shall keep out.*
> *Afterwards, I would certainly oppose Arjuna and*
> *kill him";*

That might perhaps be his Jealousy and envy. Duryodhana accepted all the conditions put forth by Bhishma and appointed Bhishma as the General.

* * *

The Views of Balarama

When Balarama, the brother of Krishna visited the Pandavas in their military camp, Yudhishtira, Krishna and others gave him a warm welcome. He had come to Kurukshetra not with happiness but with a heavy heart as the war had been declared. He was overwhelmed by greed, anger and hatred because the peace settlement had not been achieved as desired.

He addressed Yudhishtira and said:

> *"O! Yudhishtira! A total destruction would be the result of the war. Duryodhana however much he may be bad, he is the same to us as Pandavas. I am not for taking sides in their foolish quarrels. How could Krishna and I in opposite camps? So I have decided to keep myself out of this war."*

This was the decision taken by Balarama.

* * *

The Story of Rukmini

Bishmaka was the king of Vidarbha. He had five sons and only one daughter namely Rukmini. She was a beautiful and a charming woman. When she heard of Krishna and his reputation, she fell in love with him and wanted to marry him. It was an unquenchable and divine love!.

Although most of her relatives approved this proposal, her eldest brother Rukma persuaded his father not to accept the proposal of his sister Rukmini's in marrying the ruler of Dwaraka. Rukma wanted to give his sister in marriage to Sisupala, the king of Chedi. When she was put in this predicament, she was completely perplexed; she was in a sad plight and did not know what to do. After some deep thinking, she decided to find a solution.

Accordingly, She chose a learned Brahmin and sent him as her emissary to Krishna in Dwaraka. He conveyed to Krishna, Rukmini's sad plight and her request explaining in detail the whole situation.

The gist of the letter is:-

"Worshipful Master! My brother has decided to marry me to Sisupala, the king of Chedi. As a part

of wedding ceremonies, I will be going to the temple
of Parvathi. That would be the best time for you to
rescue me. If you do not help me, I will put an end
to my life so that I may atleast try to join you in my
next birth"

After her prayer, when Rukmini came out of the temple, she could notice the chariot of Krishna and immediately, she ran to him and mounted the chariot and escaped.

Rukma wanted to wreak vengeance against Krishna by killing him. There was a fight between Rukma and Balarama in which Rukma was defeated.

* * *

Bhishma, the commander-in-chief of the Kaurava troops gave an inspiring talk to Duryodhana and others. He also praised the warriors in his troop, their skill and strength.

Next Karna became the subject of their discussion. Bhishma said that Karna does not deserve to be called a great warrior. He had already stripped his divine armour. He had earned the curse of Parasurama also. In his hour of need the power of his supernatural weapons would also fall away. Above all, he is haughty and over- confident.

Karna got wounded and retorted saying that the respectful old Bhishma always insulted him because of his hatred and envy. Although Duryodhana pacified him in so many ways, Karna was adamant and kept out during the first ten days of the battle until the Grandsire Bhishma fell wounded. He, however, went to Bhishma and asked for forgiveness and blessings. Then he proposed Drona for the leadership of the Kaurava troops. When Drona also fell, Karna took over the command of the Kaurava troops.

* * *

Krishna Announced the Rules of War

Everything was set for the battle. The warriors on both sides prepared themselves ready for their action. They were keen on observing the traditional rules of war. The rules of warfare in Kurukshetra battle are worth knowing.

1. Each day the battle would be over at sunset.

2. Both the hostiles would mix freely like friends outside the battlefield.

3. Single combats would only be between equals.

4. Those who leave the battle or retired would not be attacked.

5. A horseman could attack only a horseman, not anyone on foot.

6. The charioteers, Elephant riders and Infantry men could fight only with their equal partners of the same kind.

7. Those who seek quarter or surrender should not be attacked.

8. No disarmed warrior and no retreating warrior who has lost his armour should be attacked or killed.

9. No non-fighting attendants who were blowing conches and beating drums could be attacked.

These were the usual, traditional rules that were followed solemnly and sincerely by both the Kaurava and Pandava groups.

Bhishma addressed his leaders under his command saying that they were given a golden opportunity and asked them to fight bravely and attain name and fame. He further exhorted them saying:

"The dogma of kshatriya is not to die of disease or old age in his bed but to die on the battlefield"

Yudhishtira on the other side said to his troops:

"No doubt, the enemy force is large and our army is smaller. So our tactics should be concentration rather then deployment. So let us arrange our troops, in **needle formation.***"*

As soon as the address of Bhishma had come to an end, the Princes in charge of battalions ordered the trumpets to be sounded and the war was to begin. Each leader in the battlefield on the side of Kauravas had his own flag for avoiding confusion.

Bhishma's flag had palm tree and five stars as a symbol. Aswatthama's flag had the lion's tail. Drona had ascetic's bowl and the bow on his golden coloured flag. Duryodhana had the cobra on his flag. Kripa's flag had a bull painted on it. Jayadratha's flag carried a wild boar. In short, it was a colourful pageantry of flags fluttering in the air beautifully.

* * *

Yudhishtira Seeks Benediction

Before the actual commencement of action in the battlefield, there was, as usual, a tense situation. Both the sides of the army were arrayed in proper order. All on a sudden, to the amazement of both the armies, Yudhishtira put away his weapons, dismantled his armour, got down from the chariot and proceeded towards the commander of the Kaurava forces.

Krishna, Arjuna and Yudhishtira's brothers were all perplexed. They were also a little agitated. They could not clearly understand why Yudhishtira was proceeding towards the enemy's side in such an unusual way. But Krishna who could easily study the hearts of men could understand and said:

> "Dear Partners, Yudhishtira is going to the elders to seek their benediction before fighting in the war"

The warriors in Duryodhana's army thought that Yudhishtira was coming to have a truce or a peaceful settlement.

But Yudhishtira proceeded straight to the Grandshire, Bhishma. He bent himself low, touched his feet, saluted and spoke:

"Most revered Grandshire! Grant us permission to begin the battle. Although you are incomparable and unconquerable, we humbly seek benediction before commencing the fight"

The grandshire appreciated Yudhishtira for his most honourable and worthy conduct and blessed him whole-heartedly.

Then Yudhishtira went to Dronachariar, circumambulated and bowed and asked for his blessings who also blessed him.

In the same way, he approached and obtained the blessings of Kripacharya and uncle Salya.

Everything was set ready for the battle. Arjuna requested Krishna to drive the chariot as he wanted to see the army of the enemy. In response to Arjuna's request, Krishna drove the chariot to the centre of the battlefield; When Arjuna looked at both the opposing armies, he felt all on a sudden trembling with emotion.

Arjuna, grief-stricken as he was, addressed Krishna:

"O Krishna! Now when I see my own kith and kin, I hate taking part in this war. I do not crave for winning in the war by killing so many people"

Tears rolled down from his eyes.

Krishna was surprised to see a change in his outlook.

"O Arjuna! what has happened to you? You have got a big crisis in your life. As a good archer and also as a great warrior, you must rise up to the occasion and act courageously. A hero like you in a war-field should never turn your face away, when the battle is to begin. Arise Arjuna and take up your arms and fight bravely in the battlefield".

"Fight with joy and without any inhibition; Attain fame, pursue your traditional path of your ancestors and follow".

* * *

Gitopadesh

Krishna still saw Arjuna in low sprits. So he decided to motivate him. So Krishna thought that it was the right time for him to deliver the sermon of **'Karmayoga'** to Arjuna.

Arjuna could himself realize that he was both diffident and indifferent; as a result he had no boldness which was not the true nature of a 'kshatriya' warrior. A Kshatriya should never withdraw himself from participating in a war; So he asked Krishna to give his advice.

Arjuna also felt and said:

> *"How can I fight against my own Grandshire Bhishma, and my own Gurus? Instead of workshipping them, Can I kill them! How can I take up arms against my own kinsmen?"*

Krishna smilingly replied:

> *"Arjuna! You are pitying for those who do not deserve to the pitied. As a wise man, if you are so, do not have compassion either for the dead or the living"*

Fig 6: Krisha tells Gita to Arjuna

"All sorrow in life arises from our undue attachement. Remember, the soul is immortal. It is imperishable. It is only the body that perishes. A living person on this earth passes through many stages in life namely childhood, youth, old age and finally the last stage called death."

"By mistake or by lack of understanding you think that you are the one who kills and your enemy thinks that he is killed. Both of you are totally wrong."

"When you kill somebody, what you kill is only the body and not the soul. What has not taken birth can never die; when the soul is eternal and imperishable, how could one kill?

When a garment gets old and torn, we usually throw it away and get a new garment.

Likewise, the soul abandons the body when it becomes weak, old and ruined, and takes up a new body.

If you realize this great truth, you won't grieve at all."

*"Do your duty, Do not expect anything in return not even a reward or words of gratitude; so Arjuna! be resolute in your mind and rise up to fight. As a kshatriya, your duty is to fight;you must just fight and must not think of the fruit of your action! Success or Failure! You must treat them both equally! This is **karmayoga!**"*

"O!Krishna! what is the way to reach God"- asked Arjuna.

"There are two ways to reach God. One is by meditation and the other is duty or work for men of action."

Fix your mind on the Omnipotent and detach your mind from all desires. Then you can do your duty free from sin.

"O! Krishna! What prompts a man to commit a sin?' asked Arjuna.

"Anger and Desire prompt a man to commit a sin. These are the two greatest enemies of man!

"O! Krishna! You say you taught this to Vivasvan, Manu and Ikshvaku. Vivasvan was born thousands of aeons (period of time too long to be measured) before you came. So I am yet to understand how this was possible."

Krishna smiled and said:

> *"O, Arjuna! I have several births as you have but I know and remember all of them, while you have no knowledge of past lives; whenever there is dearth of 'Dharma' or righteousness', I take the incarnation of a human form."*

> *"I am born 'yuga' after 'yuga' to protect the good, to destroy the wicked and to establish 'Dharma" in this world."*

> *"You could choose any path to approach me. All paths lead to me."*

> *"So whatever that you do, whatever you eat, whatever you sacrifice, dedicate them all to me. You will be free from the bondage of Karma – both from the good and evil fruits of your work"*

Arjuna:

> *"O,Krishna How can I approach you by meditation? I know you are All-powerful! Where can I find you? Where do you dewell? How should I worship you? What should I offer to please you and to please myself?*

Krishna said:

> *"I dwell in the hearts of everybody, everything too! I am the Beginning, the Middle and the End – I am Vishnu, I am the Sun! I am the Moon! I am the Mind in all living things. I am the great 'Aum'. I rule over the entire universe."*

Devotion is the highest form of worship. Dedicate all your actions to me. When you worship me, I grant liberation; always fix your thoughts on me.

"Work or action should never be given up. Surrender all your attachments for the fruits of your action."

The feeling of 'I' should be erased from your mind.

Trust not the Future, Bury the Past, Live the present. Rest your Heart on the Omnipotent.

Arjuna:

When we worship you, what could be offered to you in order to show our love and devotion to you?

"One or Two leaves of Tulsi and a few drops of water would suffice to offer me!"

This is also believed to be a traditional practice. Arjuna got his great Enlightenment from Krishna, When Lord Krishna showed his **'Viswaroopa',** he also felt that he was free from his mental agony and tension. He felt light in his heart and mind. So he set out on his journey of Duties and Responsibilities and took up arms for his fight in the war.

When the battle began there were single combats between the Divisional chiefs armed with weapons of equal size and nature. There were the combats between Bhishma and Arjuna (Partha), Abhimanyu and Brihatbala, Duryodhana and Bhima.

Yudhishtira and Salya and Dhrishtadyumna and Drona.

Besides thousands of other warriors fought observing the rules of war of those days.

There was also indiscriminate fighting among common soldiers. Such *free fighting* was known as **'Sankula yuddha'**.

For the first ten days, the fight was under the command of Bhishma on the Kauravas' side.

Drona took the command after ten days.

Karna took over after the killing of Drona.

Salya led when Karna fell at the close of the seventeenth day and on the eighteenth day.

At the end of the battle many barbarous (savage) and cowardly deeds could be seen.

The battle at Kurukshetra every day was very much the same; Any graphic description of the fighting and killing may be dull and monotonous. Still the battle at Kurukshetra is the most significant event in the great epic Mahabharata. It we ignore this event, one cannot fully understand the heroes of the epic on the crowded stage.

There were fighting for eighteen days before the great war culminated and they decided at the end many important issues in the epic.

* * *

The Beginning of the War at Kurukshetra

The First Day's Battle

Dushasana commanded the Kaurava army while Bhimasena did the same on the Pandava side. Abhimanyu however, was deputed to fight against Bhishma. The Kaurava forces, seeing this, surrounded Abhimanya on all sides. But Abhimanya the brave son of Arjuna and Subhadra showed his superb skill which perturbed the Kaurava troops. Noticing this strategy, the Pandava warriors gave protection to Abhimanya which made the Kauravas to be more defensive.

In a different scene, Prince Uttara of Viratnagar came to attack Salya mounting himself on an elephant. King salya was the ruler of Madra kingdom which was located around the river Vitasta also known as Jhelum which is in modern Pakistan.

Queen Madri of Pandu was Salya's real sister. So he was the maternal uncle of Pandavas. When he learnt that war was likely to break out between Pandavas and Kauravas, he organized a strong army and came to the camp of Pandavas.

Prince uttara, sitting on an elephant attacked Salya so fiercely that all the four horses of Madra were killed. Salya grew angry and aimed a spear at the Matsaya prince which killed him and he at last fell down from his elephant and died.

On seeing this, his elder brother Sveta came opposite to Bhishma and fought fiercely and bravely. Though he killed hundreds of Kaurava soldiers, he fell down and died. Anyhow, Kauravas had an upper hand.

The Second Day's Battle

As there was a setback for the Pandavas on the first day of the war, Arjuna and Dhrishtadyumna were cautious and they formed their army this time in the **'Krauncha Formation'**.

On the command of Duryodhana, the Kaurava army led by Bhishma attacked their enemy forces of Pandavas fiercely. The army of Pandava's side was a little shaken with fear. When Arjuna observed this, he asked Krishna to drive his chariot to the place where Bhishma was fighting. When Arjuna started advancing towards Bhishma, the Kaurava General attacked him with a volley of arrows.

Arjuna became restless and also agitated and moved forward to attack the Kaurava forces with a vengeance. Now Duryodhana felt sure that it would be difficult for them to check Arjuna's advance. In addition he took charge of another wing. He used his mace. Pandavas fought so fiercely that Duryodhana fell down. Immediately his charioteer drove him out of the field. Arjuna along with Satyaki killed the charioteer of Bhisma. The horses in fear and fury ran out of the battlefield. Bhishma also escaped in his horses.

On the other side of the battlefield, Panchala Prince, Dhrishtadyumna, Supreme Commander of the Pandava forces and eldest brother of Draupadi attacked Dronachariar first with a mace and then with a sword. But Drona wounded him with his arrows. Bhima on seeing this ran to help him. He attacked Drona and he fell down almost out of his wits.

When Duryodhana and Karna saw this, they ran fast to help the great Guru. But Bhima attacked the whole regiment and killed very many soldiers. The Kaurava army got diffident. Bhishma attempted to attack the Pandavas but Abhimanyu and Satyaki intruded. The sun set and the battle came to an end.

The Third Day's Battle

On the third day of the war, Bhishma arranged his army in **Eagle formation**. Bhishma himself led the army. The beak in the eagle formation was Bhishma. Drona and Kritavarma were the two eyes. Aswattamma and Kripa were the head of the bird, and finally this tail was filled with a huge army under Brihatbala, the king of Kosala.

On the other side, Arjuna in consultation with their commander Dhrishtadhymna arranged the Pandava army in the **form** of a **crescent**. Bheema stood himself with his army on the right side of the crescent. On the curved central body of the crescent were Drupada and Virata. At the centre was Yudhishtira with the elephant troops. On the left side of the narrow shape of the crescent were Satyaki and Draupadi's sons. Abhimanyu and his brother were also near them. Arjuna's chariot with Krishna holding the reins got stationed at the left horn of the **Crescent formation.**

When the battle began Arjuna's (Dhanenjaya's) attack was very powerful.

A counter – attack from the Kaurava's side was made against Arjuna's position. Javelins, spears and other weapons like missiles were thrown in the air against the enemies.

Sakuni with his large force stationed himself at another point and aimed at Satyaki and Abhimanyu. Satyaki's chariot was broken to pieces and he had to run and squeeze himself in Abhimanyu's chariot. They however, succeeded in destroying Sakuni's forces.

Bhishma and Drona jointly attacked Yudhishtira's forces. Nakula, Sahadeva with their brother opposed and disturbed Drona's offensive fight.

Bhima and his son Ghatotkacha fought bravely and brought havoc to the Kaurava forces. Bhishma and Drona too were shaken with fear.

When Bhishma and Drona were thus defeated, Duryodhana grew angry and found fault with them for showing partiality to the Pandavas.

Bhishma retorted saying:

> *"O crown prince! I had already given a note of caution by saying that the Pandavas are invincible. I can even now tell you that you can not defeat the Pandavas so easily as you are following an evil path where as they fight for a noble cause".*

Thus the Pandavas gained an upper hand in the first half of the day. But at the latter part of the day, Bhishma followed certain strategy and attacked the Pandavas severely. Even a great fighter like Arjuna, Bhima and Sikhandi could not do anything.

Krishna then reminded Arjuna of his pledge to kill Bhishma, Drona and Karna. Arjuna got a little upset over this remark and he asked Krishna to drive their chariot so close as to face Bhishma.

Arjuna then shot his arrows at Bhishma and broke his bows one after the other. Gradually, again a fierce fight between the two started. Krishna was greatly upset and forgetting his vow not to take up arms, he got down from the chariot in order to fight personally against Bhishma. Arjuna ran to Krishna and brought him back.

The Fourth Day's Battle

At break of dawn, Bhishma arranged the Kaurava army again. He was surrounded by Dronachariar, Duryodhana and others. The Kaurava army was thus ready for the fight.

Bhishma wanted his forces to pounce upon Arjuna and others. But Arjuna was alert and led a counter attack. Duryodhana had an evil plan and so he sent his army men to surround and kill Abhimanyu. When Abhimanyu was left alone, Dhrishtadyumna who could notice this rushed to help him.

On another front, Bhima tried to attack the Kaurava warriors who had been advancing towards Abhimanyu. Duryodhana let loose a herd of wild war-elephants but the mighty warrior, Bhima attacked the wild-elephants which ran scattered; This resulted in a wild stampede and total disorder amongst the Kaurava forces.

Bhima, however, was attacked by Duryodhana with a weapon which made him fall in a swoon for a few minutes. Ghatotkacha just then appeared on the spot and attacked fiercely the Kaurava army.

When the sun set, Bhishma ordered the closure of the day's battle as the soldiers were weary.

The Fifth Day's Battle

Dhiritarashtra, when heard about the happenings of the great battle from Sanjaya, started lamenting and he was unable to bear his grief.

> "I am like a shipwrecked man seeking to save himself by swimming in a storm – tossed ocean. I shall surely drown, overwhelmed in this sea of sorrow".

So said Dhiritarashtra. He was in great distress. The blind old king burst into tears.

Sanjaya consoled the king by saying that it was Duryodhana's own making.

> "The Pandavas fight for a just case. So they are bound to win. On the other hand your sons are wicked even though they are brave warriors. Therefore, perhaps luck does not favour them".

> "your sons, the Kauravas have done great injustice to the Pandavas. So they are reaping the harvest of their own sins. Besides they fight with certain principles of Kshatriyas".

> "Vidura, Drona, Bhishma and I advised you not to follow the wrong path but you refused to listen to good advice".

The battle commenced the next morning. Bhishma arranged his army in a strong formation.

The Pandavas' forces were also arranged equally well by Dhrishtadyumna. Bhima stood on the forward area. Sikhandin, Dhrishtadyumna and Satyaki stood behind. They carefully guarded the main body of the army. Dharmaputra, Nakula and Sahadeva guarded the rear side of the army.

Bhishma started sending his shafts against the Pandavas. The Pandavas' side suffered heavily. When Arjuna (Dhananjaya) noticed this, he retaliated by hitting hard on Bhishma.

Duryodhana could not bear this. He lost his temper and was angry with Drona. But Drona retorted and patiently said:

> "Duryodhana! We are doing our best to drive the enemies out; unfortunately, you do not know the mighty strength of the Pandavas"

Thus saying, Drona tried to pounce on the Pandavas like a hungry lion. Bhima and Satyaki prevented his advance.

It was then that Sikhandi moved forward to check them. Bhishma left the battlefield as he thought that it was below his dignity to fight against a eunuch. By noon, a good number of soldiers on both sides were killed.

Then Duryodhana deputed Bhurisravas against Satyaki who was killing the Kaurava soldiers in large numbers. It was difficult for anyone to defeat Bhurisravas as he was a famed swordsman. When Satyaki was seriously wounded, his ten sons came to his rescue but all of them were killed by Bhurisravas.

On the other front, Arjuna fought bravely and killed many Kaurava soldiers.

The Pandavas were quite happy and they shouted victoriously.

The sun set.

The fight for the day came to an end.

The Sixth Day's Battle

On the sixth day, the Pandava army was organized **in the form of a crocodile.**

On the Kaurava side, the Kauravas organized their army **in the form of a swan.**

The fighting on the sixth day was fierce and gruesome.

At the very beginning of the fight, Drona's charioteer was killed. This angered Drona and he attacked the Pandava army with greater force.

The Pandavas also fought equally well.

There were attacks on either side; also there were counter attacks.

Consequently there was an utter confusion and there was a complete disorder.

It is a fact that Disorganization and Disorder in a battle-field always ruin the Vicotry.

Both sides had heavy losses.

Duryodhana was severely wounded while fighting against Bhima at the end of the sixth day.

The sun set.

The fight came to an end for the day.

The Seventh Day's Battle

Bhishma organized his army in a different way so that his army could fight against the enemy forces effectively.

Yudhishtira also formed his army in such a way that his troops would be able to fight against the enemies effectively. The battle was fought on many fronts.

Fig 7: Pandavas headed by Yudishthira

Arjuna fought against Bhishma while Drupada fought against Dronachariar. Bhima fought against Duryodhana and his brothers while Nakula and Sahadeva fought against their maternal uncle Salya.

Drona defeated Drupada and killed his son Shankha. Sikhandhi was beaten by Aswathamma.

On the other side, Bhima wounded Duryodhana. Ambusha, a demon fighting for the Kauravas was forced to run away from the battle field.

Ghatotkacha was beaten by Bhagadutta and Salya was beaten by Nakula and Sahadeva and Salya fell down senseless.

Yudhishtira fought against Srutayu. He also killed his charioteer. This had demoralized Duryodhana's army.

Abhimanyu moved against Duryodhana's brothers and defeated them easily when he was about to kill them, he remembered Draupadi's vow to wash her hair with their blood. So he left that place and turned his attention to Bhishma. All the five Pandavas after seeing this, rushed to help him.

Soon it was sunset.

That day's battle came to a close.

The Eight Day's Battle

When the eighth day came, Bhishma thought that he must arrange his army **in tortoise form.**

Yudhishtira also had to alter his formation to cope with Bhishma's. So he advised Dhrishtadyumna and said:

> *"Do you know Dhrishtadyumna that the enemy forces of Kauravu army is in '***Kurma Vyuha***'? you will have to have a formation suitably well so as to encounter them easily".*

Dhrishtadymna, therefore arranged their troops in **a three – pronged formation**, he being the supreme commander of the Pandava forces. He was also the eldest brother of Draupadi.

Bhima was at the end of one Prong, Satyaki at the end of another Prong and Yudhishtira stationed himself at the crest of the middle division.

When the fight began, Bhima killed eight sons of Dhrishtarashtra. Arjuna had a heavy loss in the death of his son Iravan. Arjuna had this son through his Naga wife who had joined the Pandava forces at Kurukshetra.

Duryodhana has sent his rakshasa friend Alambasa who fought against the Naga warrior and killed him. Arjuna got worried and spoke to Krishna:

> *"Vidura had already advised and forewarned that both the sides would have heavy losses".*

> *"It is enough if Duryodhana gives at least five villages"*

so said Yudhishtira.

"If he does so, we will not resort to fighting"
he further said.

But Duryodhana being obstinate, refused to give even five villages.

"O, Krishna, this actually forced us to carry on this wicked, miserable sinful way".

When Iravan was killed, Ghatotkacha could not tolerate this. He fell upon the Kaurava forces ferociously. The soldiers on both sides trembled and there was fear and confusion; with the result, the formation was broken and the whole battle field was in a disorganized status.

Duryodhana made an attack on Bhima's son. The king of Vanga joined Duryodhana with his elephant force. Duryodhana fought vigorously on this eighth day battle. He killed many of the warriors on Ghatotkacha's side. Ghatotkacha threw a javelin fiercely at Duryodhana but the king of Vanga intercepted with one of his elephants and the javeline hit the elephant which died.

The anxious Bhishma sent a large force under Drona to help the Kaurava chief, Duryodhana. The soldiers attacked Ghatotkacha. Yudhishtira also was worried about the safety of Ghatotkacha and sent Bhima to his aid.

Sixteen brothers of Duryodhana died in the battle field.

At the sunset, the fight came to an end.

The Ninth Day's Battle

The battle for the day was about to begin. Duryodhana was worried about the way in which the whole fight was going to Yudhishtira's favour. He found fault with Bhishma as he was disappointed.

To this charge, Bhishma politely but sadly explained.

> *"O, Duryodhana! I am sorry to say that your vision is clouded; you are now reaping the harvest of the hatred and malice you sowed.*
>
> *I shall certainly fight truly and sincerely. But I can not do two things.*
>
> *I can not fight against Sikhandi as I would never raise my hand against a woman.*
>
> *I can not also with my hands kill the Pandavas.*
>
> *Barring these two, I will fight all the warriors opposed to you"*

Duryodhana endorsed the views of Grandshire.

The fight between Abhimanyu and Alambasa began. Abhimanyu proved his valour and Alambasa had to take a fast run on foot to save himself.

There were also combats between Satyaki and Aswathamma and between Drona and Arjuna.

Thereafter the Pandavas attacked Bhishma and Duryodhana sent Duhsasana as a help to Bhishma.

But Bhishma could fight bravely and chase the Pandavas back. As a result, the Pandava forces were completely demoralized and ran here and there.

Krishna was angry with Arjuna who was hesitant to kill Bhishma. He said to him.

> *"Arjuna! Do not hesitate to punish Bhishma. Remember the duty of a soldier. Do your duty as a true Kshatriya"*

Krishna further said:

> *"O, Arjuna! You are not fighting as you should"*

Krishna jumped down from the chariot with the objective of fighting in the battle field.

Arjuna shouted and cried:

> *"Krishna! Stop. Do not break your oath. You took a pledge that you would not use weapons in the battle field.*
>
> *This is my task. I shall shoot my arrows though I do not like inwardly to do so. Please get into the chariot and hold the reins"*

Krishna consented and the battle got resumed.

When the sun went down, the fight came to an end.

The Tenth Day's Battle

On the tenth day of the battle Arjuna attacked Bhishma having Sikhandin in front of him as a shield. It was

Sikhandin's fierce fight. His darts flew very fast and pierced the chest of Bhishma. Bhishma's anger grew wild and his eyes reddened as if they would burn sikhandin.

Arjuna was also continuously shooting arrows at Bhishma. As Bhishma did not like to attack an eunuch, rather a woman, he got down from the chariot with a sword in his hand. But Arjuna broke Bhishma's sword as well as his shield into pieces with his powerful arrows. Bhishma inwardly knew that day's war was his last fighting day.

Fig 8: Bhishma refuses to fight with Sikandi

Bhishma fell down leaning against the side of his chariot. But his body did not touch the earth because all the arrows were sticking all over his body.

Duryodhana ordered his men to bring cushions in order to give support to the hanging head of Bhishma. But the grandshire refused to accept. So Arjuna took out three arrows out of his quiver, fixed them in the ground just under Bhishma's head. Thus he provided support to the grandshire's head on their points.

Fig 9: Krishna and Pandavas (along with Narada) converse with Bhishma lying on a bed of spikes.

Then the grandshire turned again to Arjuna and said:

"My son! I am feeling thirsty. Get me some water"

At once, Arjuna took out an arrow and shot it with such a heavy force that a fountain of water gushed out of the earth. It rose high and came down so as to fall into Bhishma's mouth. It looked as if the very Ganga rose up to quench the thirst of the dying man.

"Duryodhana! Why don't you reconsider my suggestions? See how Arjuna provided me with water. Make peace with Pandavas without delay"

159

But Duryodhana was not pleased.

On learning that Bhishma lay wounded and dying, Karna ran to the spot and prostrated himself before him and with humble salutation said:

> *"O Revered Grandshire; I have incurred your displeasure for no fault of mine".*

Bhishma placed his hands on Karna's head and blessed him:

> *"you are not Radha's son, my dear! You are Kunti devi's own first born".*

Karna replied:

> *"I know that I am Kunti's son and not charioteer – born. But I have eaten Duryodhana's salt and must be loyal to him. So it is unthinkable for me to join the Pandava's side. You must forgive me and bless me".*

The Grandshire said:

> *"I am glad that you are loyal to Duryodhana who installed you as the King of Magadha. Be firm and loyal to Duryodhana. Fight your enemies as you think. You may go".*

Thus Karna got Bhishmas's blessings, received his benediction and mounted his chariot and drove to the battlefield.

Now is the time for Duryodhana to decide the choice of the next commander of the Kaurava forces. So he held a council with Karna. It was then decided with everybody's approval and accordingly Drona was appointed as the Commander – in – chief of the Kaurava army.

The Eleventh Day's Battle

Dronachariar took the command of the Kaurava army. He gave heavy losses to the Pandavas. Though it was the eleventh day of the war, for Drona, it was the first day of his command of the Kaurava forces.

Drona lad a special love for Arjuna; He loved the sons of Kunti, more especially the righteous person, Yudhishtira. When Duryodhana asked Drona to capture Yudhishtira alive, he was very happy. But Duryodhana had his own evil design. If Yudhishtira were killed, nothing could be gained much. But the anger and enmity of the Pandavas' would develop very much. That would only lead to the destruction of both the sides.

In this way, Drona again got disappointed that he could not complete his task once again.

In the meantime, Duryodhana who noticed this took Karna with him and went there. He also took with him a big regiment of war-elephants. But Bhima could drive the war-elephants which ran amuck. While running, the elephants crushed their own soldiers with their feet.

Bhagadatta, king of Pragjotisha, an ally of Kauravas was a great warrior. He rushed to the spot sitting on a war-elephant which was a well-trained animal on the war-front. This elephant twisted its trunk round Bhima's body and lifted him. But Bhima with his mace gave severe blows on the animal and the elephant ran away.

Arjuna fought with vehemence against king Susharma. At the same time, he was worried about his elder brother Yudhishtira. Suddenly he could feel the effect of two weapons flung on both-on himself and Krishna. Arjuna instantly shot three arrows which made the weapons useless. And another arrow from Arjuna forced Susharma to run away from that spot.

Then Krishna wheeled his chariot to the place where Bhima and Bhagadatta an ally of Kaurava's were fighting. Arjuna sent several arrows at Bhagadatta and his elephant and both fell down and dead.

Sakuni and his brothers appeared on the spot to fight against Arjuna. When Sakuni tried to attack Arjuna, his fatal arrows wounded Sakuni and he fled from the battlefield.

This was the end of the eleventh day's fight.

The Twelfth Day's Battle

Drona understood his failure to capture Yudhishtra alive. He also realized that it was impossible to do this unless Arjuna is separated from his elder brother, Yudhishtira.

Susharma, the ruler of Trigarta took up the responsibility of leading Arjuna away from Yudhishtira. He raised a large force and took his five brothers – Satya, Satyavarma, Satyavrata, Satyeshu and Satyakarma with him. Then they all gathered, sat before the fire and performed a 'Yagna' and took an oath either to kill Arjuna or flee in fear from the battle.

Susharma then challenged Arjuna. Being a true Kshatriya he accepted the challenge after entrusting the care and protection of Yudhishtira to Satyajita, Draupadis' brother. Krishna wheeled his chariot towards them. Arjuna fell upon them like a hungry leopard. The twelfth day fight thus developed into a gruesome fight between Susharma's forces and Arjuna.

As Arjuna was thus busy fighting against Susharma's forces, Drona commanded his army to move towards Yudhishtira. When Dhrishtadhymna, The Supreme commander of the Pandava forces and the eldest brother of Draupadi rushed to stop Drona's advance, Drona immediately drove his chariot to the other side where Yudhishtira stood.

But the vigilant and alert Dhrishtadhymna moved fast and intercepted between Dronacharya and Yudhishtira. A fierce battle took place over there. A good number of Pandava soldiers were killed. By sheer luck, Bhima saw his elder brother in danger. He came there with a number of warriors including Satyaki, Nakula, Drupada, Virata and Shikhandi and cardoned around Yudhishtira and Drona.

Ajatasatru is the name people have given to the eldest son of Kunti, who is no other than Yudhistira. The name **Ajatasatru** means a **person without an enemy.**

Arjuna was upset as Drona had agreed to join Duryodhana to help him. So he decided to be always near his brother on all days during the war.

Drona proved his skill and energy in the battle field. His rapid movement on the field surprised everyone. He came to the very place where Dhristadyumma was instructing the soldiers.

Sakuni and Sahadeva were engaged in a combat using their maces. Nakula attacked his maternal uncle Salya and made him retreat. Bhima brought havoc with his mace. He also made the Kaurava soldiers run.

This Twelfth day battle was frightening. Both the sides fought with a vengeance, Arjuna's son Abimanyu, Satyaki and king Virata fought very furiously. Abhimanyu's fight was very furious. He was boldly fighting against four top leaders – Paurava, Kritavarma, Salya and Jaidratha.

Abhimanya was able to overpower his opponent and forced them to retreat.

Kaurava forces, when they saw this, lost their courage and ran pell-mell. The disappointed Drona was searching for Yudhishtira. When he spotted him, he moved fast his chariot and went near the senior Pandava, Yudhishtira and he wanted to capture him alive. Like a lightning, Arjuna appeared on the scene. He sent his volley of arrows against his Guru Drona with perfect aim which forced Drona to retreat. Thus concluded the twelfth day's fight.

The Thirteenth Day's Battle

As usual Duryodhana found fault with Drona for showing a soft corner towards the Pandavas. Atlast Drona plainly told him that it would not be possible for him to seize Yudhishtira alive as long as Arjuna surrounded him and protected.

On the thirteenth day's fight, Drona rearranged his forces in **Lotus Formation**. Bhima, Satyaki, Dhrishtadyumna, Dropada, Kuntibhoja, Virata and with many others opposed Drona. But Drona's strategy in the new Lotus Formation paralysed all the efforts of Bhima's group.

Yudhishtira called Arjuna's son Abhimanyu and said:

> *"Dear Son! No one with us has been able to penetrate through the Lotus Formation of Drona. I am sure that you know you can do it and none else. So why don't you take up this task?"*

Abhimanya replied that he could do it as his father had instructed how to penetrate into this formation.

Yudhishtira further said:

> *"My brave son! Try to cut open this impregnable formation and open a passage for us to enter in.*

*We will protect you. So only break the formation
and the rest we will do and destroy the Kaurava
army".*

Bhimasena endorsed the proposal suggested by
Yudhishtira and said to Abhimanyu:

*"If you could break the enemy's formation
successfully and enter in, I shall follow you.
So also Dhristadyumna, Satyaki, the Panchalas, Kekayas
and the army of Matsyadesa. Once we enter
in, it will be easier for us to destroy the Kaurava
army:.*

Abhimanyu with great euthusiasm decided to plunge
into action. So he asked his charioteer Sumitra to drive fast
to that spot. The charioteer cautioned Abhimanyu against
the risks involved. But Abhimanyu thought that he could
easily fight against the Kauravas as they are only a sixteenth
part of his strength.

The Kaurava forces were annoyed when they saw
Abhimanyu's chariot fast approaching them. Abhimanyu
reached the spot. There was a bend in the formation of
Kaurava forces and soon developed into a break and thus
there was a breach in the circular formation and Abhimanyu
entered in easily. But the breach was closed by Jayadratha,
king of the Sindhus before the Pandava warriors could enter
in as they had previously planned. Thus Abhimanyu was all
alone inside the ring.

Kaurava warriors fought and opposed him but soon they fell down and died one after another. Duryodhana who noticed the great destruction caused by this young lad rushed in and opposed him. Thus he was engaged in battle.

Drona immediately sent a large number of experienced warriors who included Drona himself, Aswathamma, Kripa, Karna, Sakuni and Salya to save and protect Duryodhana. But Abhimanyu could withstand the united fight of these war veterans.

Duhsasanna roared like a lion and was determined to attack and kill Abhimanyu but he could not succeed; and he was finally driven away by Abhimanyu from the field.

Next Karna came in to attack Abhimanyu with his shafts but even his bows were broken by Abhimanyu. Thus the army of Duryodhana was routed.

The Fourteenth Day's Battle

Arjuna tok a vow to kill Jaidratha. When Duryodhana heard this news from his spies, he got scared. Immediately he informed this to Jaidratha, the ruler of Sindhu. He then prepared himself to go and save his kingdom. But Duryodhana asked him not to worry about his safety as he had already taken measures for his safety. Drona also pacified Jaidratha when he expressed his fear.

On the fourteenth day war, Durmarshana the brother of Duryodhana came to the battlefield with his army-an army of chariots, war-elephants, horsemen, soldiers and archers and began to fight and oppose the enemy. But Arjuna defeated the whole army under the command of Durmarshana.

Arjuna was bent on killing Jaidratha. Drona tried to protect him in all possible ways. Duryodhana felt shaken with worries. He ran to Drona and explained the danger to Jaidratha's life. Drona gave Duryodhana an enchanted armour to protect himself.

Satyaki was fighting at a place in the war field. He got so much tired that he went to take rest. So Dhrishtadyumna came with a section of the army to fight against Drona.

All on a sudden the sound of Krishna's shell-'Panchajanya' was heard. When Yudhishtira heard this, he was anxious about the safety of Arjuna. So he asked satyaki to go with a force to help Arjuna. Satyaki with all humility told him that he had been given the responsibility of protecting Yudhishtira, from Drona.

Yudhishtira was still anxious about his brother, Arjuna's safety. Observing his anxiety, Satyaki hurried to go for Arjuna's help. He requested Bhima to protect his elder brother Yudhishtira. As there was no information about Arjuna, he asked Bhima to find out and so Bhima also left the place to look for Arjuna.

Krishna noticed Duryodhana coming in a fury towards Arjuna. He warned Arjuna about this, alerted him and said that he must immediately shoot at Duryodhana. At first his arrows did not harm Duryodhana and could understand the secret of his enchanted armour.

Arjuna then showered his enchanted arrows at Duryodhana and defeated him. When Arjuna killed his horses and broke his chariot, Duryodhana ran away from the battlefield in order to save his life. And he deserted Jaidratha to his fate.

Dhrishtadymna tried his best to kill Drona but in vain. Shortly a fight ensued between Satyaki and Drona. Satyaki broke the arrows of Drona three times and Drona also shot several arrows at him.

Suddenly Bhima came over there, broke through the Kaurava forces and reached the very place of Arjuna and found him safe.

The war on the fourteenth day was severe. There were fierce fights between Bhima and Karna, between Satyaki and Bhurishrava and between Arjuna and Jaidratha. Besides, the Pandavas also attacked Drona several times and this made Duryodhana lose his courage.

Bhima then overcame many of the Kaurava warriors and put many of them to death. Karna then began to fight with Bhima. The fight was terrible. In the duel fight between

Bhima and Karna, both of them could show their valour and strength. At one stage, Bhima was rendered helpless without any arms. Karna remembered his promise to Kunti that he would not kill any of the four Pandavas namely Yudhishtira, Bhima, Nakula and Sahadeva.

Seeing all these situations in the war field, Krishna prompted Arjuna to help his unarmed brother, Bhima. Arjuna'a arrows made Karna run away from the battlefield once again.

Arjuna just then noticed Satyaki fighting against Bhurisravas. The fight was severe. Satyaki grew tired; Bhurisravas was so cruel that he lifted Satyaki and threw him down. When Bhurisravas was about to kill Satyaki with his sword, Arjuina shot a powerful arrow at him which cut Bhurisravas's right arm. He fell down with severe pain. It was then Satyaki picked up Bhurisravas's sword and killed him on the spot.

Arjuna thus fought bravely. He was determined to kill Jaidratha. He was able to go very near Jaidratha. He shot at Jaidratha's neck and cut off his head.

The Kauravas were very much angry and they were not ready to put an end to the fight even after sunset.

Ghatotkacha was the son of Bhima by his asura wife. When Ghatotkacha tried to attack the Kaurava forces, he killed countless men in their army. Ghatotkacha on some earlier occasions caused troubles so much that Karna decided to use the divine weapon to attack him; even though he had preserved and reserved this for using against Arjuna only. He used this now and thus Ghatotkacha was atlast killed.

Then Arjuna turned his attention to attack Jaidratha and got succeeded in killing him. His head was cut off and he died.

Drona was upset over two facts; Yudhishtira was not captured alive nor Jaidratha was saved. Krishna suggested to the Pandavas that they must use some tricks to kill their enemies, especially Drona.

Krishna suggested they must try to spread a false message saying that Aswathamma had been killed in the battlefield. Such a message would dampen the spirit of Drona and in a dejected mood, he would lay down all his weapons.

In the meantime, Bhima killed an elephant named Ashwathamma and shouted in joy,

"I have killed Ashwathamma"

When Drona heard this, he was shocked. But he wanted to confirm the veracity of this news.

Yudhishtira is a righteous person who would never tell a lie. So Drona called him and asked him about this; Yudhishtira said:

"Ashwathamma has been killed, not your son, but an elephant"

On the suggestion of Krishna, a drum was beaten exactly at the time when the concluding part of the sentence was to be uttered.

Drona so thought that his son Aswathamma had been killed. He threw off all his weapons and sat down in his chariot in a pensive mood.

Dhrishtadymma instantly cut off his head and Drona died.

The Fifteenth Day's Fight

All the three stalwart warriors on the Kaurava side namely Bhurisravas, Jaidratha and Drona had faced defeat on the fourteenth day's war. So Karna took up the responsibility of leading the Kaurava army. He had chosen Salya as his charioteer.

Arjuna chose an auspicious day to fight with Karna. Not only that, he chose to take a new regiment of able soldiers for the fight. Bhima, his elder brother led this regiment.

When Duryodhana observed this, he sent Duhsasana to help Karna. Bhima grew angry when he saw Duhsasana. Bhima could not control himself. He pounded on Duhsasana's body with his mace; He cut his right arm.

Bhima remembered Draupadi's agony when she was dragged into the court hall by Duhsasana. He began to suck the blood of Duhsasana and roared like a lion as a result of his victorious deed. In his jubilant mood, he challenged Duryodhana for a fight.

Duhsasana's murder by Bhima had affected Duryodhana very much. He could easily foresee his own defeat. Aswathamma consoled him and suggested for peace talks with the Pandavas. He addressed Duryodhana and said:

> "No more fighting; stop it; Let us put an end to this enmity. Dear Duryodhana, make peace with the Pandavas and stop the battle."

But Duryodhana being wicked and villainous, did not heed to his advice. He started attacking the Pandavas with a vengeance.

In another corner of the battlefield, there was a fierce fight between Arjuna and Karna. Karna wanted to wreak vengeance against the Pandavas. Krishna got pressed the chariot down five fingers deep in the mud. As a result, Karna's fire-shaft could strike only the top of Arjuna's helmet and it did not strike Arjuna's head. Arjuna lost his temper and sent countless arrows at Karna. As if Karna's fated hour had come, the left wheel of his chariot got stuck up in the earth.

Karna appealed to Arjuna requesting him to wait. He also said that it would be unfair for Arjuna to attack him when the wheel of his chariot got stuck up.

As Krishna could not hear this, he said:

"Hey, Karna! How could you talk about fairness when you did not even feel for Draupadi and kept silent when she was dragged by her hair by Duhsasana to the court hall? You kept silent when the Pandavas were about to be burnt alive. Was it fair to poison Bhima? Was it fair on the part of Duryodhana and Sakuni to cheat Yudhishtira in the game of dice? Was it fair to kill Abhimanyu when he was without his arms?"

Karna felt that he was insulted and he grew furious. In a fit of anger, Karna tried his best to kill Arjuna but in vain. Krishna suddenly shouted to Arjuna and said:

"Arjuna! Waste not your time. Aim at your enemy and kill Karna"

Though Arjuna's mind was wavering for sometime, he rose up to the occasion and sent an arrow and cut off Karna's head who fell down and died.

The Sixteenth Day's Battle

Karna's death affected the mind of Duryodhana very much. He went to Kripacharya his Royal Priest and sought his advice. When the priest found fault with him for his pursuance of the path of evil, and his stubbornness, Duryodhana did not relish.

Then a fight between Yudhishtira and Salya ensued. It was a duel fight and a fierce battle. Yudhishtira gave a fierce blow to Salya with his sword and Salya fell down and died.

The fall and end of Salya prompted all the brothers of Duryodhana to attack the Pandavas. They all surrounded Bhima and began to fight with him But Bhima with his supreme strength killed all the brothers one by one.

Bhima then challenged Duryodhana and killed him after breaking his left thigh. Thus he fulfilled his vow of revenging Duryodhana.

In another part of the battlefield there was a grim battle between Nakula and Sakuni. Sakuni was a great fighter and he had come with his son Uluka. When Sakuni had the upper hand over Nakula, Sahadeva came over there.

Sahadeva who came to help Nakula, had fulfilled Nakula's oath by killing Sakuni's son Uluka. Sakuni was upset and he fought with Sahadeva vehemently. When Sakuni started fleeing from the field, Sahadeva threw a Javelin which cut Sakuni's head. That was Sakunis death. The fall of Sakuni left Duryodhana deserted and he was left alone and there was nobody to help him.

The Seventeenth Day's Fight

Thus Duryodhana was left alone and the Pandavas were looking for him everywhere.

Gandhari and Kunti had come and reached Kurukshatra. She knew that her son Duryodhana had been left alone to face his opponents, the Pandavas. She could also remember Bhima's oath to break Duryodhana's left thigh. So she wanted to protect her son and so she called her son Duryodhana and said:

> "Duryodhana! Go to the nearby Saraswathi river and have a bath; Make your presence before my eyes without wearing any garment on the whole of your body. I will remove the piece of cloth on my eyes and cast a look at your body. This will make your body impervious to any blow by any weapon."

Krishna who had come to know of this wanted to scuttle Ghandari's plan. So he went to the river side and made fun of Duryodhana and said:

> "Duryodhana! Don't you feel ashamed of going before your mother in this manner? Atleast cover your loins in this manner with some thing."

So Duryodhana covered his loin with banana leaves. Thus the whole body of Duryodhana became impervious; of course except the loin part of his body concealed with banana leaves.

Duryodhana then hid himself near a lake. The Pandavas who were searching for him, found his hiding place and asked him to come out. Then they challenged him to fight with them, one by one.

The duel took place for a long time. Bhima made use of this opportunity and gave him a heavy blow on Duryodhana's left thigh and broke his bone. He fell down and Duryodhana was left there.

Balarama who came there was angry with Bhima. He said that Bhima could not be called a warrior when he did not observe the norms of war-code.

Krishna explained in detail all the atrocities committed earlier by Duryodhana including his forcing Draupadi to sit on his left thigh.

Krishna further said:

> "Don't you remember that Duryodhana killed Abhimanyu, our sister Subhadra's son when he was unarmed? Karna attacked him from behind. Don't you remember how Panchali (Draupadi) was abducted by Jaidratha on Duryodhana's request when she was alone in a hut during Pandava's exile?

Ashwathamma, Drona's son when he learnt how Bhima had broken Duryodhana's left thigh, he could not control his anger. Seeing Duryodhana's pathetic condition lying half dead, Ashwathamma told him that he would take a pledge to kill the Pandavas.

Duryodhana was pleased with the consoling words of Ashwathamma and he appointed Ashwathamma, son of Dronachariar his army's general for the eighteenth day's fight.

Kripacharya tried all methods and words of advice to prevent Ashwathamma from doing these evil acts, but in vain.

Ashwathamma with his determination got into the tent; when the inmates were asleep, he killed Drishtadymna and all the warriors who had come from Panchali. He then made an attempt to kill all the five brothers of the Pandava group. But none of the five was there. So Aswathamma killed all the five sons of Draupadi one by one.

Then the three Kauravas-Aswathamma, Kripachariar and Kritavarma killed the Pandavas whomever they came across. They also set fire to all the tents of Pandavas.

When Duryodhana heard all these particulars especially the killing of all the five sons of Draupadi, he was quite happy and died somewhat in peace.

The Eighteenth Day's Fight

It was in the next day Yudhishtira and his brothers learnt all that had happened on the previous night. They were all in sadness. Atleast, they thought, eight Pandavas were alive then-Five Pandava brothers, Draupadi, Kunti and Uttara.

Draupadi was very much grieved. The Pandavas consoled her. Then they searched for Aswathamma. At last he was found in the ashram (hermitage) of saint Vyasar. Aswathamma got frightened. He took a blade of straw in his hand and chanted some mantras and said:

"Fly and kill any child in the womb of any Pandava woman."

The very next moment, the straw transforms itself into a sword, moved rapidly to the place where Abhimanyu's widow, Uttara was sitting; Of course, Uttara was in the family way.

Luckily when Krishna noticed this enchanted sword, he diffused its power and Krishna could save Uttara and her baby.

Bhima became furious and uncontrollable. He fought with Aswathamma and could make him accept his defeat.

Aswathamma took out a precious stone from his forehead and presented it to Draupadi who gifted it to Yudhishtira.

In this way, the fateful war of the Mahabharatha came to an end with the defeat of Aswathamma. When Dhritarashtra learnt this, he was also in great grief. He cursed Aswathamma saying:

"You wicked man! You have destroyed the very lineage of Hastinapuram"

Vidura tried to console the old blind man, Dhritarashtra. In the meanwhile, saint Vyasar came over there. He pacified the Kaurava king and said:

"Dhritarashtra! My beloved king! Everything happens according to Destiny. Treat Yudhishtira as

your eldest son and other Pandavas as younger sons.
Live in peace."

At that time, the Pandavas along with Krishna came there. First Dhrishtarashtra and then Gandhari showered their blessings on all the Pandavas. It was only then they both realized all these unhappy events occurred only because of the evil designs of Sakuni, Karna and Duhsasana.

Then the Pandavas moved and set their feet on the banks of the river Ganga where they stayed for a month in order to perform the last rites for all those dead in the war.

At the end of the 18th day Kurukshetra war, the Pandavas had a glorious victory. Yudhishtira became the emperor of the entire kingdom of Hastinapur. At such a time, generally any person who had won laurels in the war would be exceedingly happy.

But strangely, Yudhishtira was still grief-stricken over the fact that he had lost all his kith and kin. When he heard from the messenger that saint Narada had come, he went to the entrance and heartily welcomed him.

The king gave a piece of his mind especially about Karna. He had come to know the fact quite recently that he was his eldest brother. His mother, Kunti who was there narrated all the particulars about Karna's birth and how curses fell on him by saint Parasurama.

Hearing all that was said of Karna by Kunti, Ydhishtira said to Kunti:

> *"Dear Mother! How it is strange and unbelievable that you have concealed all the facts about my brother, Karna. To be frank, these facts actually are the causes of my sorrow."*

Yudhishtira was so much affected in his mind that he lost interest in everything. So he wanted to renounce all the worldly affairs and became an ascetic. All his brothers and Draupadi tried their best to prevent him from doing so. At that time, saint Vyasar arrived there. He also advised and persuaded him to accept the kingship.

Dhrishtarashtra was plunged in great sorrow. He was treated with reverence by the Pandavas. They tried all efforts to make him feel happy. They were all careful in seeing that Dhrishtarashtra was not insulted or humiliated in any manner.

Ghandari who had lost hundred sons was also treated with respect by Kuntidevi. Draupadi also assisted and rendered services to both of them with sympathy and tenderness. The royal princes who came to Hastinapura as visitors were given the same honours by Dhrishtarashtra as they did in the past. Yudhishtira advised all his brothers to give their uncle their highest regards especially when he had lost all his sons. It was only Bhima who found it difficult to forget and forgive Duryodhana, Duhsasana and Karna. Kunti conducted herself so well that she looked as if she was the embodiment of Dharma who practised dharma (righteousness) in her life.

Fifteen years passed in this way under the rule of Yudhishtira. Dhrishtarashtra being old was unable to bear the heaviness of grief in his mind. As it is laid down in the Sastras, he wanted to go to the forest and spend the last years of his life doing penance. The time has come for him and Grandhari to go and live in the forest.

Yudhishtira was greatly disturbed in his mind. He was not happy over the decision taken by his uncle Dhrishtarashtra. He persuaded his uncle so many times not to go to the forest but in vain. Saint Vyasar then entered. When he was told all that had happened just then, he said to Yudhishtira:

> *"Dhrishtarashtra has grown old. He has lost all his sons. He cannot bear his grief anylonger. Grandhari also has borne her sorrows with courage. So do not stand in the way of their wishes. The time has come for him to do penance."*

Then the Royal preparations for the Coronation of Yudhishtira were begun. Kunti's illustrious son Yudhishtira sat on a golden throne. Yudhishtira's brothers and Draupadi, Dhrishtarashtra and Gandhari, Kunti Devi, Krishna, Satyaki and the only son of Dhrishtarashtra by name Yuyutsu were also seated in their respective places of importance.

The Coronation of Yudhishtira was celebrated colourfully with all pomp and glory. The celebration was well attended by a large gathering of Royal families as well as learned religious people. The new Emperor Yudhishtira was honoured and blessed by people of all ranks. Then in a grand ceremony Yudhishtira was crowned as the king by Dhaumya a preceptor or adviser of the Pandavas.

King Dhrishtarashtra's presence was a signal honour to the new Emperor Yudhishtira. Yudhishtira also crowned Bhima as the Yuvaraja. The other brothers and his well-wishers were all pleased and honoured with appropriate positions in the Royal court.

Yudhishtira noticed Krishna in a serious mood in which he was thinking deeply over something: He asked Krishna what had made him so serious. Krishna said that he was thinking about the most respected Grandshire Bhishma who was lying on his bed of arrows. He also said that he might meet his end very soon. He wanted to meet him. Yudhishtira also expressed his willingness to meet the old Grandshire.

So, as they had decided, Krishna, Yudhishtira and the other Pandavas went to the battlefield. Yudhishtira sought his blessings and also his advice. He also asked Bhishma to tell the art of ruling over the kingdom well.

* * *

The Art of Kingship

Bhishma was pleased with his eagerness to learn **the art of kingship**. So he said:

> *"My child, Listen to me attentively. I shall narrate in detail the duties of a king.*
>
> *The foremost duty of a king is to worship the Almighty and to respect and adore the learned men and 'Acharyas'.*
>
> *A king should be a man of action.*
>
> *A king should always build up confidence in the minds of his citizens by being true to them. A king should be righteous in all his deeds, controlled and humble.*
>
> *A king should cultivate an alert mind and should never have excessive trust in anyone.*
>
> *A king should always uphold Justice and render justice to his citizens irrespective of caste and creed and religion.*
>
> *A king should be able to keep any secret of his plans all to himself.*

A king should also respect and workship Matha (Mother), Pitha (Father) and Guru (Preceptor)."

This is how Bhishma enlightened Yudhishtira on the nuances of a good ruler.

* * *

The Death of Krishna

Krishna ruled our Dwaraka for thrity-six years. The Yadava families enlarged into a large member.

It so happened that a group of saints visited Dwaraka. A prince named Samba wanted to test the powers of the saints. They wanted to test especially their supernatural powers. So Samba disguised himself as a pregnant woman and met the saints. Samba asked the saints whether the baby-in-womb was a boy or a girl. The saints were greatly perturbed and shocked. They grew wild and they cast a curse and said:

> *"You will give birth to a pestle and the pestle will be the cause of the destruction of your entire Yadhava dynasty"*

The curse came out to be true and the Yadavas fought with each other because of internal disunity. Balaraman was very much upset; he could not tolerate this kind of internal flights amongst the Yadavas and died.

In the case of Krishna, he went to the forest on a particular day. He lay asleep when he was sitting under a tree. The soles of his feet were glittering brightly.

A passer-by who was a hunter mistook them for deer's eyes. When he shot an arrow at Krishna's feet, the arrow killed Krishna on the spot.

The whole Yadava race got wiped out and Balarama's and Krishna's death also occurred. When this news reached Hastinapura, Yudhishtira got very much upset and he decided to renounce the world.

He blessed Parikshata, Abhimanyu's son and enthroned him as the next emperor. All the five brothers and Draupadi decided to visit holy places on a pilgrimage.

After visiting many holy places, the Pandavas reached the Himalayas. A dog followed and joined them in the middle of their climbing and followed them all along. As the whole route was rugged and hazardous, one by one amongst the five brothers and Draupadi felt exhausted and died. But the dog still followed Yudhishtira.

* * *

Dharma Is the Only Unfailing Companion in Man's Life's Journey

Perhaps the great epic poet **saint Vyasar had tried to emphasize** in this particular episode **that Dharma is the only unfailing companion in Man's life's Journey.**

Thus Yudhishtira was left alone with only the dog as his companion. Yudhishtira could notice with wonder that the dog had been following him as a faithful companion. When he approached the great heights of the snow clad Himalayan range of mountains, Indra appeared before him in his chariot.

> *"Your wife Draupadi and your brothers have already come over here before you. You are late. Get into my chariot and come along with me. I have come to take you."*

Yudhishtira ascended over to take his seat in the chariot. The dog also jumped up.

Indra pushed the dog away saying that there was no place for dogs in Heaven. ('Swarga'). Yudhishtira instantly said:

"If there is no permission for the dog to occupy a seat in the chariot, I have no room either; I will not go there."

Dharma had come to test Yudhishtira and was pleased with his conduct. He (Dharma) admired his loyalty to the dog and his love for Justice. The dog then vanished. Then Yudhishtira ascended the divine chariot and reached Heaven.

There he saw Duryodhana seated on a high beautiful throne. But he could not see his brothers or Draupadi.

Yudhishtira was greatly astonished. He got so much agitated that he questioned Lord Indra.

"How could a wicked and vicious person like Duryodana get a seat? Where are my brothers and my wife Draupadi? I wish to go where they are. I do not wish to be in Heaven. What is the use of my being here away from my brothers and my wife."

"My Heaven ('Swarga') is wherever they may be. To me that is Heaven ('Swarga') and not this place."

The Angels in Heaven when they heard this from Yudhishtira, they said:

"If you may so desire to be with them, you may go immediately."

So saying the Angels ordered a guide to take Yudhishtira to the place where his brothers and wife were.

As they proceeded, the way by which they went along became dark all on a sudden and there was darkness everywhere and the whole place looked very strange. He waded through slippery paths spilled with blood. The entire path was strewn with bones and dead people's hair. Worms were rolling and wriggling everywhere and there was a smell of an abnoxious stench in the air. He saw mutilated human bodies everywhere.

Yudhishtira was preplexed and horrified.

"How far and how long should we go along this dirty path? Where could we find my brothers and my wife? Explain to me?"

The messenger said:

"If you may so desire, we shall turn back."

The foul smell of the place was so sickening that for a moment, Yudhishtira intended to go back.

But just then familiar voices were heard lamenting.

"O, Dharmaputra, do not go back! Be here atleast for a few minutes. Your presence gives us great relief. When you were entering in, you have transformed the whole air into one of fragrance, sweetness and purity. Your presence has given us a soothing comfort. So stay here and do not go back."

Yudhishtira was surprised to find that the lamenting voices mostly were Karna's, Bhima's, Arjuna's. Draupadi's, Nakula's and Sahadeva's.

191

He was also a little agitated and said:

> *"What sins have these souls committed to be here in this Hell? What good deeds did Duryodhana do to occupy a place in Heaven?"*

Yudhishtira lost his temper so much that he spoke to the angel-guide and said that he preferred to stay there where his brothers were. The Angel-guide conveyed this to Indra.

Then Indra and the God of Death ('Yama') appeared before Yudhishtira. As soon as they came, the darkness was cleared and the frightful sights were also removed. A sweet fragrant breeze had begun to blow.

The God of Death ('Yama') spoke to Yudhishtira.

> *"Dharmaputra! Yudhishtira! I have tested you thrice. The first test was in the form of a dog. The second test was when you chose to remain in hell at the request of those suffering in hell. The third one was when you were to see your brothers and wife suffering in hell, you did not swerve from the path of Dharma. You showed this when you preferred to stay here, with those suffering, in Hell. None of your kith and kin was put to suffering. It was just designed to test you. This is not hell at all. Do not grieve. We are, in fact standing in Heaven only; Just look at Narada who is also here."*

Yudhishtira was delighted to hear the soothing words of the Death- God (Yama). So he gave up his mortal frame i.e. human body and assumed a divine form. This was a glorious transformation. All the human weaknesses like Jealously, Hatred, anxiety and enmity have gone away. He was in perfect peace and happiness. All his brothers including Karna, his elder brother, Draupadi and the sons of Gandhari- all assumed the heavenly form.

Thus ended the great epic Mahabharata!

* * *

Glossary

Abhimanyu	:	Son of Arjuna and Subhadra. He Married Uttara, daughter of King Virata.
Acharya	:	A learned teacher
Achuta	:	Krishna is also called Achuta
Airavata	:	Indra's Elephant, white in colour.
Ajatasatru	:	A Person having no enemy; another name/title given to Yudhistira.
Akshayapatra	:	A wonderful vessel given by the Sun-god to Yudhistira that gives an unending supply of food.
Amrit	:	'Amirtham', tastiest food of the Gods.
Arundati	:	The sage, Vashista's Wife
Aswametha Yajna	:	A horse is sacrified for this yajna.
Aswathamma	:	son of Dronacharya – a supreme. Commander of the Kaurava's army.
Balarama	:	Elder Brother of Sri Krishna

Bakasura	:	A wicked Rakshasa (demon) who pounced upon people, kill them and eat their flesh. Bhima killed him and relieved people from distress.
Bhagadatta	:	a king on the Kaurava side
Bharadwja	:	a rishi (sage)
Brahma	:	creator of the universe.
Brahmastra	:	an astra or a missile; a powerful and an irresistible one given by Lord Brahma.
Brihanalla	:	an assumed name of Arjuna while serving at king Virata's court in a disguised form.
Bhima	:	One of the brothers of Pandavas who was hefty and and strong and as powerful as the strong wind supposed to have been born of the wind-god.
Bhishma	:	He was the eighth child of king Shantanu and Ganga.
Bhurisravas	:	a powerful king on Kaurava's side.
Bibhatsu	:	another name of Arjuna meaning a hater of undesirable acts.
Chandala	:	a person belonging to a degraded caste.

Chitrangada	:	Shantanu's elder son whose mother was Satyavati; He was the heir to the throne of Hastinapura.
Chitrasena	:	A Kaurava Warrior.
Devadatta	:	Arjuna's conch.
Devavrata	:	One of the sons of Shantanu and Ganga who was later known as Bhishma.
Dharmagranthi	:	Nakula's assumed name at Virata's Court.
Dhananjaya	:	One of the names of Arjuna.
Dhrishtadhyumna	:	Brother of Draupadi; Supreme commander of Pandava's army.
Dhritarashtra	:	Son of Vichitravirya and Ambika born as a blind child; Father of Duryodhana.
Dharmaputra	:	The son of Yama; Yudhishtira was also known as Dharmaputra.
Draupadi	:	Daughter of king Drupada, king of Panchala; she was married to all the five Pandava brothers.
Drona	:	Son of Bharadwaja, married a sister of one Kripa and a son born to them was Aswathamma.

Drupada	:	King of Panchala, father of Draupadi who was the wife of the Pandavas.
Duhsasana	:	Duryodhana's brother who dragged Draupadi pulling her by her hair.
Duruvasa	:	a sage
Gandhari	:	Dhritarashtra's wife, Kauravas' mother.
Ghatotkacha	:	Son of Bhima born through Hidimbi, a Demoness.
Hastinapura	:	Kauravas' Capital City.
Ilavla	:	a demon
Indra	:	King of Gods
Iravan	:	Arjuna's son by a Naga wife
Jarasandha	:	a powerful king of Magadha killed by Bhima in the war.
Kanka	:	An assumed name of Yudhishtira while serving in the court of Virata.
Karna	:	Son of Kunti and the Sun-God; a disciple of Parasurama – also an adopted son of Radha and Athiratha foster – parents; He was also known as Radheya.
Kichaka	:	Brother of Sudeshna, the Queen of Virata; Commander-in-chief of Virata's army. Kichaka made advances to Sairandhiri

(Draupadi); to wreak vengeance; Bhima (Valala) in the disguise of a woman killed Kichaka.

Kripacharya : Aswathamma's Uncle.

Kritavarma : A Yadava warrior fighting on the side of Kaurava army.

Kunti : daughter of Sura; she was adopted by Kuntibhoja and was named Kunti. Sage Duruvasa taught her a divine mantra through which she gave birth to a son (without marriage) born with divine armour and ear-rings; so she put the child in a sealed box and threw it into the river and this child was Karna.

Kunti- Madri : Two Queens of king Pandu who gave birth to three and two sons known as Pandavas. The sons were called, Yudhistira, Bhima, Arjuna and Nakula, Sahadeva.

Lopamudra : Sage Agastya's wife.

Madava : Krishna had numerous names – one was Madava; Madhusudana, Kesava, Govinda were the other names.

Matali : Indra's Charioteer

Nakula	:	One of the brothers of Pandavas
Nandini	:	Vashista's divine cow.
Nara	;	Arjuna or Dhananjaya
Panchajanya	:	Krishna's conch
Prabhasa	:	The Vasu who stole the divine cow of Vashista.
Pritha	:	Mother of Karna, the name Pritha was Kunti's before her marriage.
Purochana	:	An architect who built the wax palace.
Radheya	:	Son of Radha, another name of Karna.
Rajasuya	:	A sacrifice by a king to be entitled as an emperor.
Rishyasringar	:	A sage
Sahadeva	:	One of the brothers of Pandavas.
Sairandhri	:	A female attendant usually employed in female apartments.
Sakuni	:	Duryodana's uncle a villainous character; a Master of the game of dice.
Salva	:	A friend of sisupala who besieged Dwaraka to avenge Sisupala's Death.
Sanjaya	:	He is the narrator who tells blind Dhritarashtra a minute-to-minute progress of the war.

Sankula Yuddha	:	A sort of disorderly fight without adhering much to the rules of war.
Santa	:	Wife of sage Rishyasringar
Santanu	:	King of Hastinapura, father of Bhishma.
Satyajit	:	A Panchala prince who stood by Yudhistira so that Yudhistira can not be easily taken as a prisoner by Drona.
Satyaki	:	A yadava warrior,a friend of Krishna and the Pandavas determined to defeat the villainous Duryodhana.
Satyavati	:	A fisherman's daughter whom king Shanatnu loved and married; she later became the queen.
Sikhandin	:	A girl turned man, a warrior on the Pandava side. He was Drupada's son.
Sisupala	:	King of Chadi, killed by Krishna during Rajasuya Yagna.
Subhadra	:	Wife of Arjuna, Sister of Krishna; she was aslo the mother of Abhimanyu.
Sudeshna	:	Queen of Virata
Sumitra	:	Abhimanyu's Charioteer

Sveta	:	A son of king Virata who died by Bhishma's arrows.
Upaplavya	:	A place in Matsya Kingdom where the Pandavas lived after their exile of 13 years.
Valala	:	An assumed name of Bhima in the Court of Virata; There he worked as a cook.
Vanaprastha	:	A person giving up his worldly responsibilities and retiring to the woods with his wife to lead an ascetic life. The stay and living in the forest is called Vanaprastha.
Varanavata	:	A forest in which Pandavas stayed in wax-house.
Vashista	:	A sage who threw his curses on the eight Vasus to be born in the world of mortals as son of Ganga and Shantanu.
Vasudeva	:	Krishna is also known as Vasudeva
Virata	:	King of Matsya
Vyasar	:	Son of Sage Parasara who compiled Vedas.

Yama : God of Death, God of Dharma whose son was Yudishtira.

Yajna : A Sacrifice.

* * *

CPSIA information can be obtained
at www.ICGtesting.com
Printed in the USA
BVHW041157280623
666441BV00002B/403

9 781646 786305